Contemporary's

Lifescenes Lifeskills

Reading and Writing for Comprehension

Calvin R. Stone
Penny Fitzgerald
Janet Weitz

Project Editor
Karin Evans

CONTEMPORARY BOOKS

a division of NTC/CONTEMPORARY PUBLISHING COMPANY
Lincolnwood, Illinois USA

Library of Congress Cataloging-in-Publication Data

Stone, Calvin R.
    Contemporary's lifescenes, lifeskills.

    1. English language—Text-books for foreign speakers.
2. Readers—Life skills.   3. Life skills.   I. Fitzgerald,
Penny.   II. Weitz, Janet.   III. Title.   IV. Title:
Contemporary's life scenes, life skills.
PE1128.S846   1986   428.6′4   86-8837
ISBN 0-8092-5103-5

ISBN: 0-8092-5103-5

Published by Contemporary Books,
a division of NTC/Contemporary Publishing Company,
4255 West Touhy Avenue,
Lincolnwood (Chicago), Illinois 60646-1975 U.S.A.
© 1990, 1986 by NTC/Contemporary Publishing Company

7 8 9 0 DBH 17 16 15 14 13 12

Editorial Assistants
Julie Landau
Ann Upperco

Editorial Director
Caren Van Slyke

Production Editor
Patricia Reid

Illustrator
Guy Wolek

Art Director
Georgene G. Sainati

Art & Production
Princess Louise El
Arvid Carlson
Lois Koehler

Contents

To the Reader

This book is called *LifeScenes* because it is made up of short scenes from the lives of seven characters. In each chapter, you'll find out how the characters are facing different challenges and changes in their lives.

Every few pages, usually after you read two scenes, you'll come to a section called "Questions About the Story." The exercises in these sections have three purposes:

1. They will help you follow what's going on in the story.
2. They will help you strengthen your reading and writing skills.
3. They will point out issues raised in the story and give you a chance to think about them and apply them to your own life.

So as you can see, the exercises are a very important part of the book.

There are answers to most of these exercises in the back of the book. However, not all the questions have one right answer. Sometimes the answer key will give possible answers to questions, but it will indicate that it's fine if you don't agree or if you have answered differently. Sometimes the answer key will not give any answers at all. Then you're totally on your own to express your ideas about an issue.

In *LifeScenes*, you will find out what the characters think about, what they feel, whom they love, and what their lives are like. But as you know, life is not that simple. You might wonder how much money they make and how they make ends meet. How do they budget their money? Or you might wonder if they live in rented apartments or if they own their homes. How did they go about finding their homes? In addition, you might want to learn some of these money management and other consumer skills yourself.

That's why *LifeScenes* has a companion book called *LifeSkills*. If you work in *LifeSkills* at the same time as you read *LifeScenes*, you'll find out how the *LifeScenes* characters learn skills like managing money, using credit, buying a car, and even starting a business. And you'll practice applying these skills to your own life.

But most of all, we hope you enjoy reading *LifeScenes*.

To the Instructor

You are holding *LifeScenes*, the reading comprehension/writing volume of the LifeScenes/LifeSkills series. *LifeScenes* combines a high-interest story with reading comprehension and writing skills development.

The readings in *LifeScenes* are followed by exercises designed to help students understand the story and do some writing about it. The scope and sequence chart on page vi gives the range of reading skills that the exercises are designed to reinforce.

The exercises fall into four major categories: "Main Ideas and Details," "Reading Between the Lines" (inference), "Vocabulary," and "Application."

We encourage you to use the "Reading Between the Lines" and "Application" exercises to promote discussion among your students. We hope these exercises will give students a better understanding not only of the story but also of their own lives. Discussion among students will be particularly helpful preceding the writing activities.

The writing exercises in this book are intended to allow students to express their ideas. They are not intended to be formal essay assignments. Research has shown that students' learning and understanding in any curriculum area can be reinforced by writing. We hope that the casual introduction of informal writing assignments in this book will help your students learn to express their ideas on paper. Encourage your students to simply write down their ideas without worrying about grammar and mechanics. Then assist them in finding ways to improve their written communication, focusing on the clarity and specificity of their ideas.

The seven chapters of *LifeScenes* correlate to the seven chapters of *LifeSkills*, its companion volume. The two books can be used together, although both stand alone. In *LifeSkills*, Bob, Carol, Rita, and Djuan learn a variety of consumer and business-related skills. The story line in *LifeScenes* provides a natural setting for the introduction in *LifeSkills* of such topics as balancing a checkbook, budgeting, using credit, buying a car, buying a home, opening a small business, and filling out tax forms. In the exercises, students practice math and life skills, and then apply these skills to their own lives.

READING SKILLS SCOPE AND SEQUENCE CHART

	Chapters						
	1	**2**	**3**	**4**	**5**	**6**	**7**
	Exercise Numbers						
MAIN IDEA AND SUPPORTING DETAILS	1–3 5–7 9–11	2–4 7 11–13	1–2 6–7 10–11	1–2 5–6 8–9	1–3 6–7 9–10	1–2 5–6 10	1–3 5–7
Summarizing			6			6	
Cause/Effect					7		
Restating	3, 7	4, 13	7		6		
Sequence	10		2	6	10	10	6
INFERENCE (Reading Between the Lines)	4, 13	1, 9 10	8	4* 10	4*, 8	7, 9 11*	2, 8
Inferred Main Idea		1				9	
Compare/Contrast		10					
Point of View	4			4			
Characterization	13	9	8	10	8	7, 11	8
VOCABULARY	12	8	3, 12	3	11	3	4
APPLICATION	8	5–6	4–5 9, 13	4*, 7	4*–5 8, 12	4, 8 11*	

*listed as both Inference and Application

CHAPTER 1
The Characters

SCENE 1
Bob

A fly soared through the open window. It cut quickly to its left and headed up the row of cabinets that lined the wall. It ignored the rows of English textbooks that Ms. Nicholson kept on the shelves. At the end of the room it went into a power dive, swooping gracefully at the last minute to avoid smashing into the blackboard.

At this point the fly appeared to take note of Ms. Nicholson. She was discussing a book by Ernest Hemingway with her class of high school juniors and seniors. Banking lightly to the left, the fly slowed and appeared to move into a landing pattern above the teacher. It circled, hovered for a brief moment, then dropped into Ms. Nicholson's hair. The teacher flicked the fly away with her hand while she continued to talk to the class about symbolism.

The fly didn't appear to care that Ms. Nicholson not only had prevented it from landing but perhaps also had threatened its life. Undisturbed, it headed almost straight for the ceiling and changed its direction. Then it soared directly over the heads of the students sitting in the third row from the window.

Bob, who was sitting in the last chair in the third row, had been watching the fly from the moment it entered the room. In fact, he had concentrated so hard on hearing the fly that he hadn't heard a word Ms. Nicholson had said about Hemingway. Bob's mind wandered. He was impressed with the freedom that the fly had, and he couldn't help but contrast that freedom with his own. "For all practical purposes, I'm bolted to this chair," he thought. "If I were to try to get up or even scratch my foot, I'd first have to get permission to move from Ms. Nicholson . . . and why should I need permission to move? I'm an adult."

He thought again about being an adult and checked his watch to see what month it was. Yes, his birthday for this year had passed. If he subtracted the year he was born from this year, he got eighteen. "So what am I doing here?" he asked himself. "How could my eighteenth birthday have come and gone and left me practically bolted to a chair in English class on a beautiful spring day? And why should an adult like me have to answer to another adult like Ms. Nicholson?"

As the fly beat a path down the third row, Bob realized that in an instant it would be in range. He'd once seen Muhammad Ali grab a fly out of the air on the Johnny Carson show. As if it had a mind of its own, Bob's hand flicked toward the fly. Even before he realized what he'd done, he knew he'd made a mistake. Ms. Nicholson's head moved ever so slightly in his direction. She continued talking about Hemingway, and Bob braced himself for the question he knew she'd ask. To prepare for the question, he tried to concentrate on what the teacher was saying at the moment. But he couldn't. His mind wandered again.

"A minute ago she took a swipe at the fly," he thought. "She probably didn't even know she did it. But then I didn't really do it on purpose either. Is she wrong to go after me for doing something she just did? It would certainly be wrong if she knew she did it. But what if she doesn't realize that she did it? I think my father is that way, too. I hear him talking to the other men about what a stud and a boozer he was when he was young. But he's always on my case about those same things. His mind must work by storing items in separate compartments. One compartment thinks it's OK for him to brag about all the hell he raised when he was my age. But then he puts his mind in the 'How to be a good father' compartment and comes down on me like a ton of bricks. He can be such a turkey. I can't wait to get out from under him. . . ."

"Bob," said Ms. Nicholson, "can you tell the class what Hemingway had in mind in the scene where Jake puts a log full of ants into the fire?" Her eyes turned on him after she'd asked the question. "That's real good," he thought to himself. "The classroom is her fireplace, and I'm one of the ants."

Bob stared defiantly back at Ms. Nicholson as he had done all year. He said nothing. She didn't seem to know what to do about his stare. So she rather quickly answered her own question and went on with the lesson.

Bob relaxed for a moment, thinking he'd done as well as he could under the circumstances. But when the bell rang, he made a beeline for the school's Washington Street exit. He'd get some fresh air and find his friend Paul. To hell with his math and physical education classes.

SCENE 2
Paul

Paul was startled when Bob knocked on the door. He bounded out of the rumpled bed and headed for the door. Halfway there he realized that he was in his underwear. It was two o'clock in the afternoon, and Annie wasn't home yet. But the knock wouldn't be Annie anyway because she had a key. So who was it? The police?

"Just a minute," he yelled through the door. One of the legs of his blue jeans was inside out, and he stumbled as he tried to get them on.

"It's just me," Bob said through the door.

Once his pants were on, Paul pulled at the piece of tape that covered the nail hole in the door. Peering into the hole, he could see nothing. "Who is it?" he asked.

Bob laughed and took his thumb off the outside of the nail hole. He tried to look into Paul's room. He discovered another eye looking straight out at him.

"Are you alone?" asked the voice from inside.

"Yeah."

The door opened a few inches, and Paul stared through the crack while he took off the safety chain. "I thought you were at school," said Paul.

"I was. But I decided to cut out. Where's Annie?"

"Not home yet, but she'll be here soon."

The room was in its usual state. Paul's clothes lined one end of the room, hanging from nails that he'd pounded into the wall. Many of Annie's clothes were packed in cardboard boxes, but the clothes that she'd worn recently were piled on top of or hanging over Paul's clothes.

Paul pushed the breakfast dishes off to one side of the plastic kitchen table. Except for the bed, the table was the only major piece of furniture in the room. He sat down. Bob walked past Paul to a hot plate that sat on a cast-iron radiator. He turned on the hot plate and took a pot into the bathroom to get some water. "You got coffee?" he asked.

Paul lit a cigarette. "Yeah. Get enough water for two cups," he said. He put a tape into a tiny tape deck sitting on the shelf above the table. The tape deck was actually made for a car. It was wired to a twelve-volt battery that lay under the table next to a small battery charger. There were eight or ten other tape decks all over the room. They were Paul's specialty. He took pride in the fact that he could be standing outside a locked car with nothing but his tools and three minutes later be on his way home with a stereo.

"You remember Ms. Nicholson, the English teacher?" Bob asked. Not waiting for a reply, he went on. "Today she was talking about a book where a guy takes a log that's full of ants and throws it in a fire. The ants didn't stand a chance. Their only hope would have been to get out of the log before the guy put it in the fire. But you know, ants have to live someplace. If they'd lived in a different log, the guy might have taken it for the fire."

"Hey man, there's a simple answer to this problem," said Paul. "It's like I've been telling you all along. If you're an ant, you don't live in a human being's woodpile. If you do, you're gonna get burned. The system'll get you sooner or later.

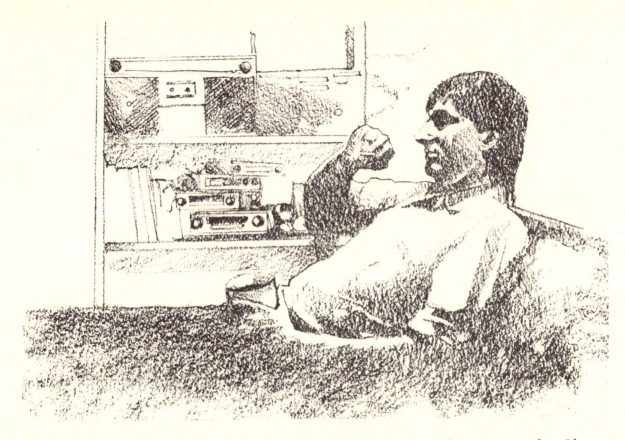

You gotta learn to use the system and take from it without being part of it. If you become a part of it, you can kiss your freedom good-bye."

"Better believe it," said Bob. "I felt like I'd been bolted to my desk at school. Is that why you dropped out?"

"Yeah. I felt that way. Why doesn't everybody just get off other people's cases and let everybody else alone? One hundred or two hundred years ago people moved west. They didn't have schools or rules or police. They had freedom. They could stop and build a house and call the land their own. And if they wanted to be with other people, they could form a town. And they could make things and sell them without the government telling how it should be done. And then if they didn't like what happened, they could move on and start all over someplace else.

"But if they ever got so that they had to depend on other people, or even on what the other people wanted or thought, then they'd had it. Good-bye freedom because you bought into the system."

The two quit talking, and Paul's thoughts drifted. He was seventeen years old and had moved out of his parents' house almost a year ago. Things hadn't been easy. His parents had not objected to his moving out except to mention that if he did, he was completely on his own. He could not come back asking for money or anything else. And he hadn't.

His hand moved to his side to check the chain that went from his belt to his wallet. He gave a tug as he did many times every day. The wallet was there and in it more than $500. That was about all he needed in life. With it he could afford to buy into a number of money-making hustles to support himself. Or if things really got tough he could buy a plane or a bus ticket to almost anywhere and start over again.

His thoughts turned to Annie. It was a little hard to imagine leaving town without her. After all, they'd been together for about six months. She worked five days a week as a waitress, working either the 6:00 A.M. to 2:00 P.M. shift or the noon to 8:00 P.M. shift. The tips were better on the later shift, and she brought home about $250 per week. She had also dropped out of high school, and the amount of money she made went to show that graduating from high school wasn't everything.

In fact, between the two of them, they could afford to move into a better apartment. But, because of Paul's "work," it was important that they not look too well off. They also had to live in a place where neighbors wouldn't question, or care about, what they did or who they were.

Paul glanced at his friend Bob, who was also in deep thought. Often in the last year he had wondered why Bob didn't leave school and start making some big money. What made Bob keep going back, day after day? The two shared so many views about school and life, but Bob was somehow different.

Questions About the Story

Throughout this book, you will be asked to take a break from your reading and complete exercises. The exercises are designed to help you understand the story, improve your reading skills, and relate the story to your own life.

MAIN IDEAS AND DETAILS

The **main idea** is the central point the author wants to make in a paragraph or passage. **Details** fill out the main idea, providing evidence and support and helping you understand the main idea.

Exercises under the heading "Main Ideas and Details" will help you to understand the important ideas in the reading and the details that support or clarify those ideas.

EXERCISE 1: Main Ideas and Supporting Evidence

Circle the letter of the choice that best completes the sentence. Then list at least one piece of evidence from the story that supports your answer. The first one is done for you as an example.

1. Bob doesn't like school because

    a. his teachers tell him that he isn't very smart

    b. other students in class pick on him

    (c.) he is not free to do as he pleases

    d. he's much too old to be in high school

    Evidence: *"I would have to get permission from Ms. Nicholson to scratch my foot. Why should an adult like me have to answer to another adult?"* (page 2)

2. Bob feels that his father

    a. doesn't like him

    b. expects Bob to be better than he was

    c. is fair and easy to live with

    d. was a goody-goody when he was young

Evidence:

3. Bob does not get along with Ms. Nicholson. We know this because

    a. he is never in class

    b. she never calls on him

    c. she likes the girls in the class best

    d. he often stares her down

Evidence:

4. Paul makes a living by

    a. stealing

    b. waiting on tables

    c. working the night shift at a factory

    d. taking Annie's money

Evidence:

5. Paul explains his life-style by saying that

    a. people need other people to be happy

    b. he wishes he could live in the distant future

    c. rules and laws destroy freedom

    d. good neighbors are important

Evidence:

6. Paul doesn't want to move to a better apartment because

    a. Annie likes it where they are

    b. he doesn't want to draw attention to himself

    c. he gets free rent where he is

    d. he can't afford to

Evidence:

EXERCISE 2: Matching

Match the details in the left column with those on the right. Place the letter of the matching detail in the blank.

_____	**1.** Bob	**a.**	a stud and a boozer
_____	**2.** Bob's father	**b.**	English teacher
_____	**3.** Hemingway	**c.**	character in book
_____	**4.** ant	**d.**	Annie's take-home pay
_____	**5.** $500	**e.**	Annie
_____	**6.** Paul's roommate	**f.**	in the log
_____	**7.** Jake	**g.**	in Paul's pocket
_____	**8.** $250	**h.**	eighteen years old
_____	**9.** Ms. Nicholson	**i.**	author
_____	**10.** nail hole	**j.**	in the door

EXERCISE 3: Recalling the Story in Your Own Words

In a few sentences, answer these questions about the story in your own words.

1. Bob thinks that his father's mind has two compartments. What are they?

   a.

   b.

2. Describe Paul by answering these questions.

   a. Where does he live?

   b. What does he believe is about all he needs in life?

   c. What did his parents tell him when he left home?

READING BETWEEN THE LINES

To complete exercises under the heading "Reading Between the Lines," you will often need to make **inferences**. When you make an inference, you identify an idea that is suggested but not directly stated. The answers to "Reading Between the Lines" questions will not always be directly stated in the reading.

EXERCISE 4: Point of View

When you describe a character's **point of view**, you are trying to see the world through the character's eyes. How would things like personality, age, occupation, or family situation affect what the character thinks and feels?

In this exercise, you'll think about the story from different characters' points of view. Answer the following questions in a few sentences by imagining that you are "in the character's shoes," having his or her experience. Use a separate sheet of paper.

1. The story describes an incident in Ms. Nicholson's English class from Bob's point of view. Now consider the incident from Ms. Nicholson's point of view. How do you think Ms. Nicholson would describe Bob?

2. Paul tries to talk Bob into quitting school. What do you think is Paul's motive for doing this?

3. How does Paul think people should live? What makes him think this way?

ANSWERS ARE ON PAGES 173-74.

SCENE 3
Liz

A row of run-down booths lined one wall of the Candy Hut. Opposite the booths was a counter lined with high stools. To the rear of the shop was a large open area where there were a jukebox, pinball machines, and electronic games. Young people from a nearby high school crowded into the Hut on school days from eight o'clock in the morning until at least six in the evening.

Liz entered the Hut at approximately 10:15 A.M. on virtually every school day of her senior year of high school. She'd wander down the row of booths looking for either an empty spot or a friend to spend part of the next two hours with. If no booths or friends were available, she'd take a seat at one of the stools that lined the counter.

Behind the counter was a woman in her early sixties, named Shirley. She was always there, and, as far as anyone knew, she had always been there. On days when Liz found no other close friends at the Hut, there was always Shirley. And though she said very little, kids knew that Shirley listened and understood. In fact, Liz and several others counted Shirley as one of their best friends.

Liz and Shirley presented an interesting pair. Shirley was old. In her face, her walk, and her way of dressing, one sensed that she had struggled through life, perhaps always working in jobs like the one at the Hut.

While Shirley could be soft and understanding, she could also be hard as nails. Nobody crossed her. When she told even the toughest students to leave the Hut, they were on their way out the door before she said another word. It wasn't so much that anyone was afraid of Shirley. It was more that everyone respected her. In the Hut she was the judge and the jury. Her reputation was that she was tough but fair.

Liz, on the other hand, was seventeen, almost fifty years younger than Shirley. Her finely cut face, her manner of moving and talking, and her clothes immediately gave away the fact that her family had money as well as class.

While Shirley blended into the atmosphere of the Hut, Liz stood out. There was some mystery about why Liz chose to spend time at the Hut. A certain kind of student hung around the Hut during school days. Many of these "Hutters," as the jocks and some of the teachers called them, were cutting class. Most were also known as freaks or "burnouts." Almost all saw themselves as being at the bottom of the totem pole in school.

Liz was an exception because she seemed to be able to move freely between the different groups of students in and around the school. That was part of the mystery. Unlike most of the Hutters, Liz could run with the jock crowd. She probably would have been chosen a cheerleader if she'd bothered to try out, and she was treated with great respect by her teachers.

Once Shirley had tried to solve the mystery when she and Liz were talking alone at the end of the counter. "What brings you down here?" she'd asked. "Do you cut classes like the rest of them?"

"Not really," said Liz. "Sometimes I cut classes, but usually I'm just here between classes."

"You know, I can usually tell who the class-cutters are. If I know kids should be in school, I chase them out of here and tell them to get their rear ends back to school. I hate to say it after all the years I've worked here, but this place is really a waste if you don't go to school, too. Just look at the kids. They spend hours and hours here. They just horse around, talking and doing the games."

"But there's nothing else to do," said Liz. "Hutters don't get along in school. They feel like outsiders. The jocks and the brains control everything. . . . The school belongs to them. This is home for the Hutters. It's where they feel they belong."

"But what about you, Liz? When you're at school, do you feel you belong?"

"Well, I do and I don't. They treat me OK, but even so, it bothers me. Last week they had a pep rally in the gym. They had a queen and king and their courts up on stage. Ten or twelve jocks were up there in tuxedoes, and the girls were in strapless dresses . . . and then there's the rest of us. Two thousand kids in the audience screaming and applauding those jocks. It's like the rest of us are there only to make the jocks feel big and important. But then a jock won't even talk to a Hutter if they see each other on the street. So you know, Shirley, if I had to choose between being a jock and a Hutter, I'd be a Hutter. At least the Hutters don't use other people to make themselves feel important. I guess I'll always be one to root for the underdog."

SCENE 4
Carol

Driving down the street on her way home from work, Carol could see that her apartment was dark. She looked again at her watch and saw that it was almost nine-thirty. Her parents must have gone to play bingo after work.

The thought of being alone in the apartment was appealing because she could sink into a chair, read the newspaper, and not have to talk to anyone. She could turn on the TV to get rid of both the quiet and the loneliness.

She gathered up her purse and school notebooks and made a dash from the parking lot into the apartment. She opened the door. "Mom, I'm home." The only answer was dark silence. She went from room to room turning on the lights—"To hell with the electric bill." She stopped in front of the full-length mirror in her parents' room. There stood an attractive young woman. "And on the verge of adulthood," she thought to herself.

"You look a hell of a lot better than you feel," she said out loud. It had been a hard day and, for that matter, a hard week. Each day had seemed to creep by at a snail's pace. But suddenly the week was gone as if it had never happened. For far too many weeks and months, her life had consisted of school, work, and evenings by herself or with just her parents. Her father had once said that they were a working class family. She'd asked what he meant by that. "Well, for me," he said, "it means you dig the ditch . . . to earn the money . . . to buy the bread . . . to make you strong . . . to dig the ditch."

That little saying of her dad's had been lurking in her thoughts for much of the day. The image it brought to her mind was that of being strapped to a treadmill that required you to use all your energy just to stay in the same place.

It wasn't that there was anything especially wrong with school or work or even living with her parents. The problem was that she had no idea where it would all lead—or even whether it was leading anyplace different at all. For all she knew she might end up working side by side with her parents at the plant. Maybe the best that she could hope for would be to get married, own a house down the street or on some other street just like theirs, and play bingo on Friday nights after work like her parents did.

The thought was not satisfying. It was even a bit frightening. What was more, she hadn't had a date for more than two months. The thought of being alone on such a treadmill was far more frightening than the thought of sharing even a miserable life with someone else.

But even in the embarrassed smile that was reflected back from the mirror, Carol thought she saw traces of strength and confidence. As she turned down the hallway, she concentrated on keeping that image firm in her mind.

SCENE 5
Ted

Ted stood at his locker almost as if he'd been frozen to the spot. A chill ran though him as he asked himself what he should do during the next hour. He realized that he was trembling. Until recently the question had never arisen. When Ted wasn't in class, he could almost always have been found hanging around the school cafeteria with the football players and wrestlers. He'd been one of *them*, one of the jocks.

But that was before the accident. The broken hip ended his participation in high school athletics. Things were not the same when he came back to school to begin his senior year. He went back to the same tables in the cafeteria. But almost immediately he felt like an outsider. The talk there was almost always about football. Practice had begun without Ted, two weeks before school had started. Then there were the stories about what team members did together after practice. And there were wild stories about the team's first road trip. Ted found it harder and harder to be involved in the social life at the tables. And, by the same token, his friends slowly left him out of their lives.

But there was a certain moment when Ted knew that he didn't belong with his former friends and teammates. He approached their table as he had for several years and took a seat near the end. He suddenly realized that the conversation had stopped the moment he sat down. His mind raced to find something to say that would get the group talking again, but he had no confidence in anything he might say. He felt only fear. It wasn't that the group would laugh at him or make fun of his talk. That's what they did to each other, and that's what made a guy part of the group. Ted's real fear was that they would ignore anything he said—as if he had never spoken. He'd seen that done to others many times, but he'd never imagined that it could happen to him.

Ted sat in a stunned silence for several minutes as he and the group watched the clock or stared blankly at their notebooks. Without saying a word, he got up. He walked toward the row of vending machines at the other side of the cafeteria. The walk seemed to take forever. He could feel the group's eyes boring into his back the entire way. Without turning around, he inserted his money into the machine and pushed the lever that said fruit pie.

"My God, why did I pick fruit pie?" he thought to himself. "They call the people they're down on 'fruitcakes.' What an idiot I am."

Shielding the fruit pie from the view of the group, he tried to get it into his shirt pocket, but it was too big. Next he cautiously slid the pie down his shirt and pushed it into the pocket of his jeans. Then he felt the awful tearing of paper. The pie exploded all over the inside of his pocket. He realized then that he'd left his notebook on the table. He turned ever so slightly toward the table to see. The notebook was there, and the guys had gone back to talking and goofing off. Keeping his hand in his pocket, Ted left the cafeteria by the rear entrance. He headed outside and straight home to change his pants. He'd worry about getting his notebook later.

Questions About the Story
MAIN IDEAS AND DETAILS

EXERCISE 5: Main Ideas and Supporting Evidence

Circle the letter of the choice that best completes each sentence. List at least one piece of evidence to explain your answer.

1. Young people like Shirley because

    a. she listens to them and understands them

    b. she lets them get away with a lot

    c. she acts and looks younger than her age

    d. she sometimes gives away candy and cigarettes

Evidence:

2. Liz could be described as

    a. a freak or a "burnout"

    b. a girl who wants to date jocks

    c. someone accepted by different types of students

    d. a daddy's girl

Evidence:

3. The mystery about Liz is

    a. where she got so much money

    b. why she hangs out at the Hut

    c. whether she ever goes to class

    d. how she got to be a cheerleader

Evidence:

4. Carol hopes that her parents won't be home because

    a. they frighten her

    b. she never talks to them anyway

    c. she wants to be alone

    d. they are supposed to be at work

Evidence:

5. Carol begins to compare her life to a treadmill because

   a. her boss is critical of her

   b. she hasn't had any dates recently

   c. it doesn't seem to be leading anywhere

   d. digging ditches is very hard work

   Evidence:

6. Ted begins to feel that he is not part of his old group because

   a. they tease him

   b. they beat him up

   c. the coach has cut him from the football team

   d. they ignore him

   Evidence:

EXERCISE 6: True or False

Indicate whether the following statements are true or false by writing a *T* or an *F* in the blank.

____ **1.** At the end of each school day, Liz goes to the Candy Hut.

____ **2.** Liz is treated with respect by her teachers.

____ **3.** Shirley is interested in why Liz comes to the Hut.

____ **4.** Liz likes to go to pep rallies.

____ **5.** Liz considers herself a jock.

____ **6.** Carol's parents are wealthy.

____ **7.** Carol works all night.

____ **8.** Ted has never been accepted by the jocks.

____ **9.** In Ted's old group of friends, making fun of someone is a sign that he is part of the group.

____ **10.** Ted puts the fruit pie in his shirt pocket.

EXERCISE 7: Recalling the Story in Your Own Words

In a few sentences, answer these questions about the story in your own words. Use a separate sheet of paper.

1. What does Liz say about these groups of students at her school?

   a. jocks

   b. Hutters

2. What is Carol's fear about her future? Why does she wish she had more dates?

3. What happens when Ted sits down at the table with the football players? Why doesn't he want them to see the fruit pie?

APPLICATION

Exercises under the heading "Application" sometimes give you information to apply to the story. Sometimes they ask you to examine ideas or issues in the story and tell how they relate to your own life. There are no right or wrong answers to the questions in "Application" exercises.

EXERCISE 8: Relating to Your Own Life

Answer the following questions in a few sentences. If you can, discuss your answers with other people. Use a separate sheet of paper.

1. Liz feels that there are social groups in her school. Ted has a problem because he is no longer accepted in his old social group.

    a. What social groups exist in your neighborhood or school? What are they called? What are the people in each group like? In what ways are the groups different from one another?

    b. Is it important to be part of a social group? Why or why not?

2. Carol's father once told her that her family is working class.

    a. What does Carol's father say it means to be working class?

    b. Do you agree with his definition?

    c. In what ways does his definition describe your life? In what ways is your life different?

ANSWERS ARE ON PAGE 174.

SCENE 6
Rita

"I love you, Mommy," said Sam as Rita tucked him into bed.

"That makes my day worthwhile," said Rita as she bent down to kiss her small son.

"What's a pain in the neck?" asked Sam.

"You're a pain in the neck," she replied. "I told you that before . . . but I love you a lot. Now it's time to go to sleep."

"Is Daddy a pain in the neck too?"

"Yes, Sam. Your father is a giant pain in the neck. Sleep tight."

"Do you love Daddy too?" asked the boy.

"Nighty night," replied Rita, ignoring the question.

Sam sometimes got right to the heart of the problem.

"I wonder if the rest of the world can see through me like Sam can," Rita thought as she left the room.

The apartment, which had been noisy all day, was now quiet. During the day she'd been responsible for Sam and three other children she baby-sat for. Tomorrow at 7:30 A.M. the children would be back, and they and Sam would be demanding her time. But for the moment, she wanted to relax and enjoy the quiet.

She sat for a moment feeling nothing, but soon she became aware of a familiar and unwelcome thought. From somewhere inside herself, she had begun to sense that she was in trouble. Though the feeling was like fear, it was different. In the past when she had been most afraid, she had immediately known the cause: a noise in the house, Sam walking toward the street, or strangers at night. She could not tie this feeling to a particular event or person. It was more fleeting and uncertain—and more troubling—than anything she'd known before.

She was tempted to turn on the television to escape from her own thoughts. "Not tonight," she said quietly. "Tonight I'm going to stay with the feeling and see where it takes me." She closed her eyes and tried to relax. For some time she thought only about her own breathing. She concentrated on the rise and fall of her chest and stomach. Soon, however, she became aware of the importance of Sam's question, "Do you love Daddy too?" The question appeared and then seemed to echo through her head, destroying the peace that she'd wanted.

The uncertain and troubled feeling swept through her again. "I'm trapped," she thought. "I feel cornered. But by what? And how did I get to this point?" As if her mind needed to escape from an approaching painful truth, her troubled train of thought ended. Her mind drifted back to a more carefree time.

Ten years before, she'd quit high school without really considering the importance of the decision. In those days she'd been in the "fast lane," hanging around with a crowd that liked drugs and music and just being together. Their future had seemed so distant that it had been beyond concern. They had lived for the moment, and the moment would have been spoiled by too much thought about where they were headed.

Rita raised her arm and looked at her watch. William could be home at any minute, she thought. Because he'd gotten out of work three hours before, Rita suspected that he'd stopped at the bar. He probably would be at least half drunk when he got home. She never knew what mood he'd be in when he'd been drinking. He could arrive with flowers or a gift and be very kind and loving, or he could be the opposite.

Rita fell asleep for a time and was awakened when the front door of the apartment opened. William was home. "H'lo," he yelled from the entry. "Got any food? I'm hungry as a bear."

Rita began to get out of her chair and realized that she was half asleep. "I'll find something for you," she said.

"What you got?" he asked, entering the room. Rita noticed that he had the funny grin on his face that appeared only when he'd had a lot to drink.

"Can I make you an egg sandwich?" she asked, getting up. As she turned toward the kitchen, William slapped her behind, hard. "I hope that was a love tap," she said, hiding her pain.

"That one was," he replied. "The next one won't be."

"Don't talk to me like that. It's the drinks."

"I'm not drunk. Just feeling good."

Rita opened the refrigerator door, looking for food for William. While she looked in the refrigerator, she also watched William behind her. "What you got?" he asked again.

"Eggs would be easiest," she replied.

"No eggs," he said, moving toward her. "Hot dogs."

"I'm sorry," she said, "I didn't get . . ."

William slapped her again, this time hitting her on the thigh.

"William," she said as calmly as she could. "You're going to have to get your own supper. I'm not going to be slapped around." As she backed away from him, William made one more threatening move toward her but then turned and looked into the refrigerator himself.

Rita went straight to the bedroom, undressed quickly, and got into bed. "I hope he's settled down when he comes to bed," she thought. "I'll pretend to be asleep."

William must not have been satisfied with two slaps at Rita. When he came to bed, Rita had her back turned toward him. She was pretending to be asleep. As he climbed into bed, William apparently decided that she wouldn't get away with turning her back to him.

This time he let her have it with his knee, right in the small of her back. Rita bolted up. She tried staring him down, but he could see her trembling.

"What do you think you're looking at!" he screamed at her. "You're really messed up!" William lunged toward her again, but she pushed at his arm and leaped out of bed. Rita grabbed her jeans and headed for Sam's room. She heard William approaching from behind. She stopped and turned to face him, this time ready to fight back. They stood nose to nose for a moment, both yelling. Rita then pushed her way past her husband and ran to Sam's room.

"What you doing?" Sam asked sleepily when his mother's shaky hand touched him.

"We have to leave now," she gasped. Picking up Sam, she headed toward the back door of the apartment. William followed her again, this time kicking at her shins.

Sam cried and clung to Rita's neck as they escaped to a neighbor's apartment. Knowing where her friend hid the key, Rita entered without even knocking. "I don't have to stay," she thought. "I'll go to my mother's. But I'll need some clothes."

Sam was still crying, but he seemed to be relieved when he was told that he was going to his grandmother's.

"Grandma Shirley?" he asked.

It wasn't the first time that Shirley had been awakened by Rita in the middle of the night. She knew exactly what to do. She took Sam and held him close while she got money to pay for the cab. Seeing that Sam was safe, Rita allowed herself to collapse on the couch.

When Shirley returned, she sat across from Rita and cuddled Sam. She had no trouble imagining what had happened.

"What am I going to do?" Rita asked.

"Was he after you again?"

"It wasn't quite as bad . . . but I can't live this way. What am I going to do?" she repeated.

"I'll kill him," Shirley said. Sam's eyes opened, and he stared up at his grandmother. When she noticed that Sam knew what she was saying, she said, "I was being funny. Grandma's a sweet old lady who loves Sam and his mama. I don't ever want you hurt."

"You love Sam," he said. Then he closed his eyes and was asleep.

"You don't take any more from him," Shirley said to Rita. "I don't care if you love him or not, you don't ever let him hit you again."

"He can be so loving, and then within minutes he can turn . . ."

"He's got a bad problem."

"Maybe it is me, Mama. I didn't have much food in the house, and he was hungry."

"Don't you dare blame yourself. He's a worm!"

Rita was surprised to hear her mother become so critical of William. In the past it had seemed that Shirley had tried not to take sides.

"Enough is enough," continued Shirley. "The man should be arrested for what he's done to you and Sam."

"How would you feel if I got a divorce?" Rita asked.

"Relieved—you know I don't believe in divorce, but the man's got a terrible problem and you can't go on living with him."

"But Mama, I don't see a way out. I've never had a good job, and I didn't finish school. How would I live?" Again, Rita began to experience the feeling of being trapped, but for the first time she could connect it with a real problem. "I can't live with him, but I can't live without him," she said.

Shirley got up. She pushed Rita's feet aside and sat next to her on the couch.

"You're going to have to get tough like your old mama," she said. "You got no choice, honey. We're going to have to dump that jerk. I'll be with you every step of the way. From now on he answers to both of us."

"But how am I going to live?"

"I didn't raise you to be weak. And I didn't raise you to need a man so bad that you couldn't make it on your own. Tomorrow you've got to get him out of your house and out of your life."

"Let me sleep on it," Rita said. "I don't know if I can do it."

SCENE 7
Djuan

Sitting at the head of the small kitchen table, Djuan led his family in the evening meal prayer. After thanking God for the food which they were about to eat, he ended the prayer with the words, ". . . bless America and bless my family. Amen." Looking up from the table, Djuan saw that Tessa was not looking down. She was gazing directly at him. "Tessa, did you pray?" he asked.

"I heard you, Papa," she said, "and I wish and hope for all the things that you pray for. But I was thinking that we work very hard for all that we have."

"We must thank God for what we have," said Djuan. Tessa lowered her eyes and silently began to eat. Djuan noted a sense of independence in Tessa's remark that he found both attractive and somewhat frightening. "My girls are growing up too fast," he said to the family.

"They grow to be Americans," said Yulanda, Djuan's wife. "In America children do not listen to parents."

"We listen. Tessa hears and I hear," said Marissa, Tessa's eleven-year-old sister. Carlo, the baby of the family, pushed at his food, and Yulanda put another spoonful of rice into his small mouth.

Djuan smiled at Marissa. "She likes so much to please her Papa," he thought. Djuan's smile grew wider as he looked around the table. Marissa was still a child, rather thin, with short hair. Even though she'd had her ears pierced and wore earrings, strangers often thought that she was a boy. This was not the case with Tessa, who had long hair. She was two years older than Marissa and had become an attractive young woman.

Yulanda, who was Djuan's second wife, did not resemble his daughters. Though only ten years older than Tessa, she had a heavier body and carried herself like an older woman. Djuan, who was almost forty years old, had a finely cut face and thick black hair speckled with gray.

Recently the family had moved into a trailer owned by Djuan's cousin, who had lived in America for more than ten years. Though the rent was more than they'd paid in the housing project, it was a place of their own, or almost their own. Djuan had planted a small garden, built a shed for tools, and taken great pride in the perfect patch of grass between the trailer and the street. Tonight he'd roll in the grass with Carlo. Afterward he and Yulanda would sit in lawn chairs and watch the sun go down while Tessa and Marissa played with the neighborhood children.

"We are lucky to be in America," he'd tell Yulanda, but as always she would not reply. Djuan suspected that because she missed her family and because she still had trouble with English, she was not happy. But he and the children were happy, and Yulanda would have to be satisfied with that.

Djuan and Yulanda sat in silence as the girls played. From down the street a car appeared, pulling a trailer loaded with furniture and boxes of clothes. The car slowed and then stopped in front of Djuan and Yulanda. The driver got out and waved to Djuan but at first said nothing. "How are you, my friend?" said Djuan as he approached the car.

"Things are not good," replied the man. "Since I was laid off, I cannot pay the rent. We must move. . . . I will find work down the road."

"I am sorry."

"Could you help with money for gas?" asked the man. Djuan reached for his wallet and handed the man a twenty-dollar bill. "You are a friend," he said, turning to get back in his car.

Djuan returned to his chair next to Yulanda. "You worry," she said.

"The man lost his job," he replied. "It is hard for many. We are very lucky to have work and family and this wonderful home."

Questions About the Story
MAIN IDEAS AND DETAILS

EXERCISE 9: Main Ideas and Supporting Evidence

Circle the letter of the choice that best completes each sentence. List at least one piece of evidence to support your answer.

1. When Rita was in high school, she was

    a. concerned about graduating and going on to college

    b. a jock

    c. not interested in the future

    d. arrested for stealing

    Evidence:

2. When Rita goes to bed, she

    a. reads a book

    b. pretends to be asleep

    c. goes to sleep

    d. watches TV

    Evidence:

3. When William comes home, he is

    a. drunk and hungry

    b. loving and kind

    c. tired

    d. carrying roses for Rita

Evidence:

4. Djuan and his family live in

    a. an apartment

    b. a housing project

    c. a rented trailer

    d. a house they own

Evidence:

5. Djuan's children consist of

    a. two sons and two daughters

    b. one son and two daughters

    c. three daughters

    d. three sons

Evidence:

EXERCISE 10: Sequence

Number the following events in the order in which they occurred in the lives of the characters.

Rita

_____   **a.** Rita fell asleep.

_____   **b.** Rita went to Shirley's house.

_____   **c.** William slapped Rita.

_____   **d.** Rita pretended to be asleep.

_____   **e.** Rita tucked Sam into bed.

_____   **f.** Rita began to feel troubled.

_____   **g.** William got into bed.

_____   **h.** William told Rita she was messed up.

Djuan

_____   **a.**   Djuan's family moved to a trailer.

_____   **b.**   Djuan and Yulanda were married.

_____   **c.**   Marissa was born.

_____   **d.**   Tessa was born.

_____   **e.**   Djuan planted a small garden and built a shed.

EXERCISE 11: Matching

Match the character on the left with the description on the right. Write the letter of the correct description in the blank.

_____	**1.** Carlo	**a.**	baby-sitting is her job
_____	**2.** Djuan	**b.**	doesn't seem to believe in praying
_____	**3.** Tessa	**c.**	Djuan's second wife
_____	**4.** A cousin	**d.**	wants to please her father
_____	**5.** William	**e.**	almost forty years old
_____	**6.** Shirley	**f.**	owns the trailer
_____	**7.** A neighbor	**g.**	the baby of the family
_____	**8.** Rita	**h.**	asks some tough questions
_____	**9.** Marissa	**i.**	hits his wife
_____	**10.** Yulanda	**j.**	borrows $20
_____	**11.** Sam	**k.**	Rita's mother

VOCABULARY

EXERCISE 12: Synonyms

> **Synonyms** are words that have almost the same meaning. For example, a synonym for *wide* is *broad*. A synonym for *cheerful* is *pleasant*. Sometimes short phrases make good synonyms. If you can't think of a synonym for a word on your own, you can look up the word in a dictionary. Usually a synonym will be part of the definition.

On the next page are some lines from the story. Each one has an underlined word. Think of a synonym for each underlined word. Then use your synonym in a sentence of your own. Underline the synonym in your sentence. The first one is done for you as an example.

1. Sam sometimes got right to the heart of the <u>problem</u>.
   If you weren't so stubborn, we could find a solution to this <u>dilemma</u>.

2. They and Sam would be <u>demanding</u> her time.

3. She began to <u>sense</u> that she was in trouble.

4. She could not tie this feeling to a <u>particular</u> event or person.

5. Rita <u>bolted</u> up.

6. She was <u>gazing</u> directly at him.

7. Yulanda . . . did not <u>resemble</u> his daughters.

8. Yulanda would have to be <u>satisfied</u> with that.

READING BETWEEN THE LINES

EXERCISE 13: Understanding the Characters

> Not everything you know about the characters in the story is directly stated. Sometimes you have to make **inferences** to understand the characters—you have to identify information or ideas that are implied in the story.

Answer the following questions in a few sentences or phrases. Some of them will require you to make inferences.

1. Describe the following characters by listing three things you know or can infer about each one. The first two lines are filled in for you as examples.

   a. Sam   *curious*
   _____
                   very young child
   _____

   _____

   b. William   _____

   _____

   _____

   c. Djuan   _____

   _____

   _____

   d. Marissa   _____

   _____

   _____

    e. Rita   _____

                _____

                _____

2. Djuan gives money to a man. How does he feel toward the man? What is he thinking about his own life?

3. Is Djuan a happy or sad person? Support your answer by listing three pieces of evidence from the reading.

  Circle one: happy   sad

  Evidence:

  a.

  b.

  c.

4. Why does Rita have trouble concentrating after she puts Sam to bed?

5. How do we know that Sam trusts his grandmother?

ANSWERS ARE ON PAGES 174–75.

CHAPTER 2
Declaring Independence

SCENE 1
Bob

The room looked even stranger than usual from the floor, and for a few moments Bob couldn't figure out where he was. He heard someone breathing loudly in a kind of half snore and raised himself up to see who was in bed. Paul and Annie were above him. Bob knew that they would probably sleep until noon.

Paul's clothes hung from the wall, making shadows that faded in and out of focus in the morning light. Bob drifted back to sleep and then woke up with a start. He couldn't remember if he'd called his father to tell him that he wouldn't be home. His head pounded as he tried to remember. He hadn't slept well at all. He was in Paul's sleeping bag on a rubber mat that Paul took camping, but the mat was designed to keep moisture away from the sleeping bag, not for softness or comfort.

He could just as well have gone home the night before. When he'd turned eighteen, his father had changed the "house rules," as he called them. "All I'm asking," he'd said, "is that you call and tell me about what time you're comin' in. I just don't wanna lay in bed and wonder if you got yourself killed in an accident." Unable to sleep, Bob realized for the first time that now the old man might throw him out of the house for good. The thought of being thrown out scared him because he had no plans. But at the same time, it would be both a challenge and an adventure.

He dressed and left the room without waking Paul or Annie. He had time to get some breakfast at the coffee shop before going to work. He was looking forward to the eight-hour shift at the station. He was scheduled to do a valve job on a customer's car, and the job would require concentration. With his work to think about, he could forget about the trouble he'd have with his father.

At quitting time, Bob left the station. He found himself driving aimlessly away from home. His thoughts centered on two choices. He could apologize to his father and say that it would never happen again. Or he could stand up to the old man by telling him that he was going to lead his own life and wouldn't be calling ever again.

Almost an hour slipped by, and Bob still didn't know what he should do. But without even thinking, he headed for home to face the music.

When he entered the living room, the old man didn't say a word. Instead he kept his face hidden behind the newspaper he was reading. Bob headed silently to the bathroom to shower and put on some clean clothes. "Looks like this is hard for him too," he thought to himself. When he was done showering, he dressed slowly before going downstairs.

"You forgot how to use the phone?" the old man asked, looking up from his paper.

Bob stood silently for an instant and then said, "Forgot. Well, it wasn't exactly that I forgot. I never thought about it."

"I was thinkin' about it. I was wonderin' where the hell you were. And whether you were bein' scraped off a windshield someplace or just hangin' around with some of the town junkies. One's about as bad as the other."

"Look, I'm eighteen. . . ."

"I don't give a damn how old you are. You're living under my roof, and that means you play by the house rules."

"We been through this already. You make the rules and I follow them."

"Yep. That's about the way it is," said the old man. A vein had begun to stand out in his temple, and Bob could see a muscle jumping below one of his eyes.

"I ain't gonna do it," Bob said. "I ain't gonna call you. There I am, out with friends, maybe with some girl, and I gotta say, 'Just a minute, I gotta call my old man.' Nobody else has to call."

"Look! Don't tell me that I should be like some of those other parents. Look at Paul. His parents let that puny little idiot go straight to hell. Don't hold them up as an example. You live under my roof—you check in with me. And that's not asking too much."

"Forget it. I said I ain't gonna."

"Then you're done. I'm not gonna worry about it if you're not here. You get out. Don't bother to come back if you're not gonna go by the rules."

"I'm on my way," said Bob. He went to his room and stuffed as many of his clothes as he could into a beat-up suitcase. He'd stay with Paul and Annie until he found a place to live. He'd come back when the old man was gone to pick up the rest of his things.

Bob headed for the front door without saying a word. He passed right in front of his father. "See you when I see you," thought Bob as he left. But the old man followed a few steps behind him. He stood silently by the car as Bob put the suitcase in the trunk. When Bob got into the driver's seat, the old man spoke. "Son, you're all I got left. Keep your nose clean."

"Yep," said Bob. "See you."

As Bob headed toward Paul's, he had a lump in his throat. "Free as a bird," he thought.

"But the old man was right. I should have called."

SCENE 2
Carol

Carol's part-time job at the supermarket became full-time the week after graduation. The boss hadn't really asked her point-blank if she wanted to work full-time. He'd just mentioned that he'd be scheduling her for forty hours a week during the summer and giving her a raise of thirty-five cents per hour. Carol was grateful. However, she did wonder how much she was in charge of her own life. "Is that what happens?" she thought. "Do doors just open in front of you, and you get swept through them because you don't have any other plan? Or should I stop to figure out for myself where I want to go?"

When Labor Day approached, she saw that the boss had also scheduled her full-time for September. Once again, he didn't ask her what she wanted. The store was becoming a second home to her. Mr. Frank, the boss, treated her like a daughter. Millie, the head of the produce department, ate lunch with her every day and "mothered" her. The others her age, cashiers and stock boys, were like brothers and sisters. Together they made up a small society or family in which each member had his or her job to do. And each could, at any time, call on the others for help. But it was Carol's friendship with Millie that began to take on special importance.

Millie was very proud of her grown daughter, who still lived in town. She would express her pride in small bits and pieces as Carol and Millie talked over lunch or worked side by side. "Janet was telling me," she said once, "that last night they brought three of the people from that accident on County Trunk C into her emergency room. One of them quit breathing just as they were bringing him in from the the ambulance.

"Janet was the first one to notice that he'd started to turn blue. You know, she had to do mouth-to-mouth resuscitation on him as they were wheeling him down the corridor to emergency. Can you imagine that? My kid saving someone's life! I don't know how she does it." Laughing to herself, she added, "Her old lady can't even walk down the street and chew gum at the same time."

Millie would also draw comparisons between Carol and her daughter Janet. "You're just like her when she was younger," she'd say. Or "I haven't had someone as fun as you to talk to since Janet left home." At first Carol was flattered by these remarks. It was nice that Millie thought that she was a lot like her daughter.

But a sense of doubt slowly began to creep into Carol's mind. "I'm not really like her daughter Janet," Carol thought, "at least not yet. Janet saves lives. I punch a cash register." And there was another side to Carol's doubt. If she really was like Janet, then why was she content to just punch the cash register instead of moving on to something else? Was she becoming too comfortable on the little treadmill that was the grocery store?

The summer disappeared and fall wore on. Carol was nowhere nearer to deciding if or when she could make some changes in her life. The need to make a change was there, but she couldn't quite turn the possibility into reality.

Then a minor incident set off a series of events that would change Carol's life. On a cold, snowy night in December, her old Buick failed her. At that moment, Bob was headed from the gas station where he worked to the grocery store. "God, I hope she'll be there," thought Bob. "She" was all he had to look forward to tonight.

Their exchanges at the grocery store had been short but pleasant. Bob often didn't know what to say, but he knew for sure he'd like to get to know her better. He'd often think about her during the day but couldn't hold a picture of her in his mind. Each time he saw her, she seemed to look different than he'd imagined. His thoughts turned to the loneliness of his life. It would be so different if he just had a steady girl.

"The damn thing just won't start," said Carol as she stormed back into the store.

She wondered how the store manager would react to her swearing.

"This is maddening," she thought. "Now I'll have to mess around with this car for hours or take a bus or cab home. I'll bet the buses and cabs aren't even running tonight."

"I'd help you, but I don't know anything about cars," said the manager. Carol noticed Bob walk in. She saw that his head was covered with snow.

Bob picked out his groceries, paid, and walked toward the door. He overheard Carol say, "What do I do now?" Feeling foolish, Bob butted into her conversation.

"How's it going?"

"What a dumb question for me to ask," thought Bob.

"I'm fine, but my car is dead," said Carol. "I wiped the snow away and tried to start it, but it just wouldn't turn over."

"Want me to have a look?"

They went outside. Bob opened the hood and fumbled around, but he couldn't figure out why the car wouldn't start.

"Let's give her a push. Put 'er in neutral. I've got the truck."

Starting the car was a challenge for Bob. However, the real challenge in this situation was Carol. Bob thought later that if a man had been stranded there, he wouldn't have offered help. His interest in Carol made him willing to help her start the car.

Ten minutes of work resulted in nothing but gasping sounds from the old Buick. Almost without thinking, Bob offered to reopen the station just for Carol and work on her car that evening.

Carol was tired from a day's work. She had been looking forward to a good meal at home and just resting or watching TV. Tomorrow would be hard for her. She had to work eight hours, and Saturdays were always very busy. Spending the evening at a service station was the last thing in the world she needed. On the other hand . . .

"Super!" said Carol. "Do you mean you'll push my car all the way to the station?"

She had often noticed Bob in the store during the months before. She had been impressed by his appearance. At first he had no beard, but that fall he let it grow. To Carol his light red hair and somewhat scraggly beard were quite attractive. If it had been anybody but Bob, she would have just called the garage, had the car towed away, taken the bus or a cab, and had that quiet evening at home. But because of her interest in Bob, she went to the station and got involved in repairing the car.

Carol was further impressed with Bob as he analyzed the trouble with the car. She liked his loose and easy manner of talking with her about the car. She noticed that he was rather quiet and hesitant when he talked about other subjects. Much of the conversation was not face to face because Bob was underneath the car.

"Looks like you got no ground. . . . Could you find me a ⅝ box wrench?"

"What's a box wrench?"

"Just give me any wrench that's ⅝. You like working at Eagle?"

"It's OK. I really like having money. You seem to know what you're doing under there. Do you think I'll be able to drive this old wreck home?"

"Hope so."

Each time Bob emerged from under the car, his face and clothes had more grease on them. After an hour and a half of work, the car started. Both young people were tired and hungry. At that point, they decided to go out together and eat. Bob refused to accept any money for working on the car, so Carol told him that the least she could do was to buy him supper.

As Bob and Carol discussed where to eat, they decided that Carol would choose what they would have and Bob would select the place. Carol suggested pizza, thinking that Bob would not be embarrassed by going to a pizza parlor in his work clothes. However, Bob chose Gino's, a restaurant that was more formal than some of the pizza parlors nearer to the station. Carol was impressed by Bob's apparent confidence. She wondered how he would feel going into Gino's in his work clothes.

Carol noticed that Bob handled going out to eat in the same confident casual way that he worked on her car. In spite of Bob's clothes and the grease around his face and in his hair, she was not at all ashamed to be with him. In fact, she felt rather proud.

Bob, meanwhile, had come to expect people his age to play phony mating games. Carol seemed different. There seemed to be none of that phoniness in her. He once had read a story that had a character who was "earthy" and "self-assured."

"She could be like that," Bob thought. "I hope I get the chance to find out."

As the evening progressed, Bob found Carol to be strong in an attractive way. As they left the restaurant, Bob stuttered, "Are you doing anything Sunday night?" The question was hard to ask. Bob had never been comfortable asking for a date.

"What?" said Carol.

"I was wondering about Sunday night."

"I guess I didn't hear what you said."

"Well, are you busy Sunday night?"

"No, I don't think so."

"A movie?"

"Sounds good. Will you call me?"

"What number? . . . Thanks again for dinner."

As Carol drove home through the snow she thought, "You never know how bad you felt until you start to feel good." She had no idea what would develop between Bob and her, but something about the evening picked up her spirits. From now on, she would begin to change her life. Her first big change would be to find an apartment of her own. Maybe finding a new place to live would help her get up the courage and the energy to discover what she would do with her life.

Questions About the Story
MAIN IDEAS AND DETAILS

EXERCISE 1: Inferring Main Ideas

> Main ideas of paragraphs or passages are not always directly stated. However, by looking at evidence, like what people say or do or think, you can sometimes **infer** important ideas.

In the first three paragraphs of this chapter, Bob awakens in Paul's apartment. He can't get back to sleep. Below are three sentences that might describe Bob's situation. Write *T* in front of any statements that are true, and list evidence for them. Write *F* in front of any that are false. The first one is done for you as an example.

T **1.** Bob would have slept better in a bed.

Evidence: *hadn't slept well; mat was designed to keep moisture away, not for comfort*

_____ **2.** Bob is sick.

Evidence:

_____ **3.** Bob knows he might regret staying out all night.

Evidence:

Now consider the first four paragraphs of the section on Carol and continue.

_____ **4.** Carol feels that she has not taken control of her life.

Evidence:

_____ **5.** In spite of her confusion about her job, Carol is a good worker.

Evidence:

_____ **6.** Carol dislikes her coworkers at the store.

Evidence:

EXERCISE 2: Knowing the Characters

Match the characters in the left-hand column with the descriptions from the right-hand column.

_____ **1.** Bob

_____ **2.** Bob's father

_____ **3.** Janet

_____ **4.** Carol

_____ **5.** Millie

a. emergency-room nurse

b. older friend of Carol's

c. all Bob had to look forward to

d. the old man

e. free as a bird

EXERCISE 3: True or False

Mark the following statements true or false by putting a *T* or an *F* in the blank.

_____ **1.** Bob's father has set "house rules" stating that Bob has to call and tell his father what time he'll be home.

_____ **2.** Bob is not bothered by the thought of his father throwing him out.

_____ **3.** Bob works at a gas station.

_____ **4.** The grocery store is like a second home to Carol.

_____ **5.** Bob decides that his father is right—Bob should have called.

_____ **6.** Carol's car breaks down on a hot summer night.

_____ **7.** Before meeting Carol, Bob has been lonely.

_____ **8.** Bob is confident about working on cars and going to a restaurant, but he has a hard time asking for a date.

_____ **9.** Bob's father figures that now that Bob is eighteen he won't worry about him.

_____ **10.** Carol feels that meeting Bob is an opportunity to begin to make some changes in her life.

EXERCISE 4: Recalling the Story in Your Own Words

Answer the following questions in a sentence or two. Be sure to answer in your own words.

1. What does Bob's father say to him as Bob leaves home?

2. How does Carol get a full-time job at the grocery store?

3. Carol's coworker Millie often talks about her daughter Janet.
   a. What does Janet do that makes Millie proud?

   b. When Millie compares Janet and Carol, Carol has two reactions. What are they?

APPLICATION

EXERCISE 5: Issues Raised by the Story

Think carefully about the following questions. Write your answers in a few sentences. If you can, discuss your answers with others in your class. Use a separate sheet of paper.

1. Is Bob's father being reasonable and fair when he insists that Bob call if he won't be coming home? Why or why not?

2. When two friends share an apartment, is it reasonable for one to insist that the other call if he or she isn't coming home? Is your answer different from your answer to question 1? Why or why not?

3. What two choices does Bob have in dealing with his father? What does he choose to do? Is this the right choice? Explain.

EXERCISE 6: A Scene in Your Life

Write a short essay (one to three paragraphs) on the following topic. If you can, discuss the topic with others before you write. Don't worry too much about grammar. Think through your ideas carefully, and write so that others will understand what you have to say. Use a separate sheet of paper.

Carol wonders whether she is ever going to take charge of her life. She fears that her future will be determined by chance. Do people create their own opportunities, or is getting ahead just a matter of fate or luck?

To illustrate your answer to this question, think of an important event in your life. How much of your success or lack of success at that time was due to luck? How much was due to your efforts? Explain.

ANSWERS ARE ON PAGE 175.

SCENE 3
Liz

"Liz," her mother said, "we'd like to talk to you about next year."

Liz had known for weeks—even months—that sometime her parents would begin such a conversation. "Oh, God, here we go," she thought. Actually the topic of what she would do after high school had been raised several times before, but never in such a formal way. And she never had to talk to both her father and mother at once.

It wasn't that they would gang up on her or that she would have trouble dealing with them. On the contrary, Liz enjoyed her parents. The anxiety she felt today had little to do with her relationship to them. The problem was in her own head. Her parents only wanted to know what she wanted to do during the coming year. She had no answer for them because it seemed so closely tied to whatever she wanted to do with the rest of her life.

Liz's thoughts drifted. Earlier in the summer she had been certain that she would attend the University next year, but since then things had become more confusing. The confusion had surfaced during the three weeks she spent at a wilderness camp in Oregon.

Liz had boarded the train to Oregon thinking that the three-week camp would be a brief and pleasant experience. She felt she would return ready to become a successful student at the University. But when she stepped off the train at the end of the three weeks, she was far less certain. The change that had occurred was difficult to explain.

The wilderness experience, for Liz, had an unexpected beginning. Even before the participants were settled at what was called "base camp," they were asked to meet at a pond six miles into the wilderness. They were to run the six miles over a winding trail. There the group leader would spell out plans for the three weeks.

Without questioning, they hastily changed into running shoes and followed their leader down the narrow path to the pond. For one mile, the group stayed together. After two miles, people began to break into two groups, one fast and one slow. Liz was lagging toward the rear of the slower group.

At the four-mile point, Liz could see nobody ahead, but she knew that part of the group was still behind, unless they'd given up and gone back. Her lungs ached and her legs told her not to go on. Her eyes filled with sweat, and soon the sweat was mixed with tears. The branches and trees around her blurred and seemed to reach out to trip her. She staggered as she tripped over roots, and she began to cry out loud. Blinded by tears, she ran into a low, hanging branch that sent her sprawling on her back. She waited on the ground for a moment. Hearing nobody behind or in front of her, she decided to keep going. Her fear of being lost in a strange place was deepened by the overwhelming thought that she was all alone.

Suddenly the thought struck her that she'd gone the wrong way. Perhaps the path that she was following would only lead her deeper into the wilderness and farther away from the others. The leader had said that the pond was six miles from base camp. Though she was not at all certain, Liz thought that she must have come five miles already. Going backward on the trail would only add to the distance. Her body told her that it would be tough enough to get to the pond even if it were just a mile. So with tears still blinding her, she stumbled forward.

The path finally began to follow a small stream. Liz hoped that the stream would soon lead to the pond. Soon she heard the sound of laughter, and to her left Liz saw several members of the group. She stopped short and tried to dry her eyes with her T-shirt before they saw her. The group leader was talking to the others and also taking off his clothes—all of them. Then he ran into the pond. Liz hesitated for a moment and then trotted toward the group. Several people looked in her direction, and without saying anything they too began to undress and head for the pond.

Liz wondered how she could undress in front of this group of strangers. On the other hand, she didn't want to sit on the shore while the rest of the group frolicked in the water. If they could do it, why couldn't she?

She sat for a moment, exhausted by the run and dazed by the need for a fast decision. She first took off her shoes, then her shorts, and finally her T-shirt. Without further thought she dashed for the pond in her underwear. As Liz's head broke above the surface of the water of the pond, she suddenly recognized the irony of her situation. She was embarrassed, even though she wasn't naked. She was embarrassed because she was still wearing her underwear. At least part of her world had suddenly been turned upside down.

The group hiked back to base camp at a brisk pace, but this time Liz was not alone. She was joined by John, a twenty-one-year-old from Marysville, Ohio, who had recently graduated from a small Eastern college. John and Liz would become partners in most of the group's tasks. The hike back to base camp was the beginning of an intense three-week romance.

A second major incident during camp seemed to Liz to create a change in her.

At the end of the camp, each member of the group was to "solo" for two days and a night. During a solo, each person had to be totally alone in the snow, glaciers, and rocks of the upper reaches of the mountains. John had been talking to Liz about meeting her and spending the two days together.

"It'll be a hell of a lot warmer and more pleasant if we're together," he said. He pointed to a place on one of their maps. "After they drop us off, we can both strike out for here. You remember this area? It's where we climbed the side of the glacier and found those ice caves just under this face. We can camp in the caves."

"I don't know," said Liz. "Somehow I think it might be best if I did two days alone."

"Aw, come on. You've got the rest of your life to do two days alone. It's the only chance we'll get to spend a long time together without having the other members of the group around."

"I know that, John. Don't get me wrong. It's very tempting. But somehow I don't want to cheat—"

John interrupted angrily, "It's not cheating. It won't hurt anyone else, and they won't even know."

"No, let me finish. I was about to say that I don't want to cheat myself. I'm not worried about doing exactly what they say or even about whether or not anybody else finds out. But I would like to know more about me, just me. So I'd be cheating myself if I spent the solo with you."

"But you'd certainly find out more about us."

"I know. But to be real honest about it, I feel like I've got to know more about me before I get any more wrapped up with you or anyone else. So, like I said, I think it might be best for me to fly on my own for two days."

"Well, look, Liz, I'm going to head out for the snow caves right after they drop me off. When you get tired of being alone out there, you'll know where to find me."

The two days had been hard. Liz dug her own snow cave. She spent much of the time burrowed in with only her head above the surface. From where she was she could see for twenty-some miles to the west. To the south was another peak where John had been dropped off. Between the peaks was the sheltered area where John would be waiting for her.

On that mountain, totally apart from other people, Liz began to feel a new sense of purpose. It wasn't something that could easily be put into words and explained to others. It was a sense of herself apart from her family and friends. It was a sense of being more totally in control of the delicate machinery that was her body and her mind. And with the sense of control there also came an almost awesome sense of responsibility. Because *she* was in control, she also had to make certain that her life had meaning and purpose. What meaning and purpose it would have was a mystery to her, but she knew that during the solo she had captured a spiritual sense of herself that she hoped would always be with her.

Later she had explained this to John, though she was afraid that he wouldn't understand and might even laugh at her.

"The test of how much control and responsibility I'm going to have was whether I could keep from going to meet you," she told him. "So my not meeting you didn't have anything to do with my feelings about you. It all had to do with my feelings about me."

"I think I know what you mean," John said. "I knew about where you were, and I probably could have found you. At first I thought I was just too proud to come looking and that I should forget the pride. But after I decided to forget about my pride, something else kept me from looking for you. I was thinking of it as a sense of independence. I must have been having about the same kind of experience you were."

"Liz, you seem lost in thought," her father said. "Can we talk about what you want to do next year?"

"Dad, I was lost in thought. And yes, I think we should have a talk about next year."

"What options do you want to consider?" he asked.

"I could go to school, either to the University or to the Technical College. But I could also work for a while and hold off on going to school until I have a better idea of what I want to be."

"You mean until you have a better idea of what you want to do for a living?" her father asked.

"Figuring out how to make a living is certainly part of deciding what I want to be, but there's more to it than that. What I really want is something that will have meaning and purpose right away. I don't want to wait four years until I'm done with college. I want it now. I told you about my solo on the mountain, and I want something that will keep that spirit alive."

"Well, you might find that spirit in some jobs. But over the long haul, going to the University would help you get into jobs that you wouldn't be considered for unless you had a college degree. That's something to think about."

"You know," said Liz, "maybe I could do both. I could go to school part-time and work part-time."

"That sounds like an interesting compromise. We can take the financial pressure off you by giving you an allowance. Let's say we give you $400 a month. Then if you find a good part-time job and don't need it all, we can make an adjustment."

SCENE 4
Ted

"I don't understand how you think you can make it on your own," his mother said. "With prices what they are today, you're just lucky to have this house to live in and a mother who's got a job . . . and you start thinking about wanting your own apartment, and with a swimming pool, no less."

"Look," said Ted, "you're not the only one with a job. I've thought about it, and I'm sure I can make it."

"I guess I'm still shocked to see you doing so well," she said. "Don't get me wrong, I'm happy about it. I just keep wondering how long it's going to last. You know, before your father and I got married, I lived at home for three years. I worked at the phone company and saved every penny so we could afford a place of our own. And believe me, it didn't have a swimming pool or tennis courts. It was just three rooms in the back of a house owned by my Aunt Fritzi. Why do you need to think of such a fancy place?"

"Well, I feel like I was down on my luck for a long time . . . ever since I broke my hip. But things are coming around, and I just don't want to wait to really get on with my life."

"It's still hard for me to see how you got where you are. I confess, there were times when you'd come home and tell me how well you were doing, and I'd think to myself that I should call your boss and see how you were actually doing. But I guess I really do have faith in you because I never called her. I don't mean to put you down about this. It's just new and hard for me to understand. Your father and I went through such hard times, and he held down two jobs for a long time. Maybe if he'd fallen into a job like yours, we'd still be together."

"I don't want to talk about that," said Ted. "You're doing OK and so is Dad. You've got a life of your own now too. I wish you'd just let go of the past. My getting a good job has nothing to do with the divorce."

Ted stalked off to his room and turned his stereo on loud enough to drown out anything his mother said. A few minutes later, the door partly opened. His mother's hand reached through to turn down the volume. The hand was then followed by her head. "You're absolutely right," she said. "I must feel like another man in my life is walking out on me. . . . But that's my problem and not yours."

"It's not like I'm leaving you, Mom. I'm not going far, and you can just pick up the telephone, you know."

"I know," she said. "And you're right. I'm doing OK."

When she left, Ted began to daydream. Though he'd never told his mother, it was also hard for him to believe that things were working out so well. At first he'd been disappointed in his job. The business education teacher had told him that he'd be doing accounting. The company he would be working for had one of the most modern computerized accounting systems in the area. Having had some experience on the school's computer, Ted had imagined himself learning to use the company's computer immediately, or at least during the first week of work. But things had not been as he'd imagined.

The company made office buildings at a factory and shipped them in pieces to other parts of the country to be assembled. Late winter and spring were the busiest times of the year in the home office. The major task during early spring was completing the plans for buildings that would be constructed during the summer.

Ted had begun work in the middle of January. The company had placed him "temporarily" in the blueprint room. This meant that he operated the machine that copied the building plans. He rolled up the plans in cardboard tubes and mailed them to the places where the buildings would eventually be constructed. The room he worked in was small and crowded. It smelled strongly of ammonia and other chemicals used in the printing process. And each day was about the same as the last. He'd arrive at work in the early afternoon to find a stack of plans, always at least a foot high. The plans needed to be reproduced, packaged, and mailed. The machine had to be fed by hand, which meant that he needed to be in the room constantly. After the first day he'd worked completely on his own in the small room, which made Ted think that the job did not require much skill. After all, how much skill could be involved if you needed only one afternoon to train for the job? The thought had been discouraging.

But Ted had forged ahead with the work in spite of his discouragement. At times, he worked past his supper break to make sure that the plans were in the mail. The offices on the first floor were dark and deserted after five-thirty in the afternoon. But on the second floor there was still light and activity. It was on the second floor that the computers were located, and they were operated sixteen hours a day.

On nights when he worked late, Ted would go to the drive-in down the road to buy supper for himself and the people who operated the computer. On these nights, they would usually eat in the computer room. Ted was, of course, full of questions about their work and how the computer was operated. They did not seem to know that he had expected to work with them instead of in the print room. Ted did not let them know directly that he'd much prefer to be working with the computer. But indirectly, Ted's interest in computer work and his knowledge about programming were apparent. Soon he was spending several hours a week just hanging around after he'd finished work in the print room and had punched out.

Noticing his interest and enthusiasm, the evening-shift workers would take the time to explain things to Ted. Eventually they got him involved in doing some of the work. In the meantime, Ted continued to work hard during the afternoons in the print room.

Eventually Ted's immediate boss, who only worked during the day, asked if Ted would like to spend a few hours a week in the computer room during afternoons when the printing and mailing were done. Ted had never mentioned to her that he'd been hanging around the computer room during the evening shift. "Yes," he said. "I'd like to get to know something about the computer and the accounting system."

The workers on the day shift were amazed by Ted's knowledge of the system. He could do some of the rather complicated work with little or no help from them.

"God, will you look at him," they said. "He seems to know just exactly what he's doing." Ted grinned and kept on working. Someday he'd admit that he'd spent several nights a week for two months learning the business, but right now he wouldn't let on. "He's a wizard," they told their boss. "Maybe you should put him up here permanently."

Later in the spring, work at the firm began to shift from planning to building. Ted's job in the print room was taken over by a high school student. Ted taught him to do the job of printing in one afternoon. At that point Ted was transferred to the accounting department, where he worked afternoons and sometimes evenings with his old friends. "God, look at him go," the day-shift workers said. "We never taught him that." Ted smiled and kept on working.

Questions About the Story
MAIN IDEAS AND DETAILS

EXERCISE 7: Main Ideas and Supporting Evidence

Circle the choice that best completes each sentence. Give evidence for your answer. Some questions require you to make inferences. The answers to these questions may not be directly stated in the story. Instead, they will be implied or suggested.

1. Before she goes to the wilderness camp, Liz expects that she will

   a. lose weight

   b. become a committed University student

   c. get herself into top physical condition

   d. have a three-week romance

   Evidence:

2. Liz is embarrassed about the nude swimming because

   a. she isn't a good swimmer

    b. other people are nude

    c. she isn't nude

    d. her boyfriend is there

Evidence:

3. The purpose of Liz's solo is

    a. to spend time alone with John

    b. to live on berries and nuts

    c. to learn to build snow caves

    d. to know herself better

Evidence:

4. Liz's most important discovery on the solo is

    a. that it is cold in a snow cave

    b. a sense of control and responsibility

    c. that she is in love with John

    d. the difficulty of surviving alone

Evidence:

5. Ted's mother is concerned about his plans to move into an apartment because

    a. she thinks Ted is too young

    b. Ted doesn't have a job

    c. she's afraid he'll drown in the swimming pool

    d. she thinks Ted wants too much too soon

Evidence:

6. Before his promotion to the accounting department, Ted has

    a. told his boss about his computer skills

    b. worked for only one week in the print room

    c. demanded a transfer so he could work with the computer

    d. learned about the computer system on his own time

Evidence:

VOCABULARY

EXERCISE 8: Antonyms

> **Antonyms** are words that have opposite meanings, such as *wide* and *narrow*.

Below is a list of phrases from the story. Each one has an underlined descriptive word. Think of an antonym or opposite word for each descriptive word. Then use your antonym in a sentence of your own. Underline the antonym in your sentence.

1.　. . . <u>brief</u> experience
　I had a <u>lengthy</u> argument with my lazy brother.

2.　. . . a <u>successful</u> student

3.　. . . a <u>wilderness</u> camp

4.　. . . a <u>winding</u> trail

5.　. . . <u>hastily</u> changed into running shoes

6.　. . . going <u>backward</u> on the trail

7.　. . . an <u>intense</u> romance

8.　. . . totally <u>apart</u> from other people

9.　. . . <u>modern</u> computerized accounting system

10.　. . . the <u>delicate</u> machinery

READING BETWEEN THE LINES

EXERCISE 9: Understanding the Characters

In a few sentences, answer the following questions about the characters in the story. Use a separate piece of paper.

1. The story about Liz describes two major incidents at the three-week wilderness camp. What are the incidents, and what effect does each have on Liz?

　a.　first incident:

　　effect on Liz:

　b.　second incident:

　　effect on Liz:

2. What does Liz decide to do after high school? Why isn't she satisfied with the idea of just being a full-time student at the University?

3. Tell why Ted gets promoted from working in the blueprint room to working permanently with computers in the accounting department.

EXERCISE 10: Compare and Contrast

> When you **compare** two things, people, or ideas, you point out similarities between the two. For example, you might compare dogs and wolves by pointing out that they have similar physical structures. When you **contrast**, you look at the differences. You could contrast dogs and wolves by saying that most wolves are wild and most dogs are domesticated.

The questions below ask you to make comparisons and contrasts based on what you read in this chapter. Use a separate sheet of paper.

1. Contrast what John wants to get out of the solo with what Liz wants. Remember, to contrast means to show differences.

    John wants:

    Liz wants:

2. Compare the reasons John and Liz do not go find each other during the solo. Remember, to compare you show similarities.

3. Contrast Ted's experiences as a young single person to those his mother had when she was his age.

ANSWERS ARE ON PAGES 175-77.

SCENE 5
Rita

At breakfast, Rita told Shirley that she had made her decision. William would have to go. "You're going to have to be stronger than he," Shirley said. "You'll have trouble. I think you're going to have to outsmart him."

Rita returned home early in the morning because she had to baby-sit for several children. As she entered her apartment, William was about to leave for work.

"Hi baby," he said. "And how's my boy, Sam? . . . Gotta go or I'll be late."

Rita said nothing about her decision to ask William to leave.

Later that morning, a delivery man rang the doorbell and presented Rita with a dozen long-stemmed roses. Tucked among the flowers was an envelope containing a small gold necklace and a note from William, apologizing for the night before. It was signed with the words "I love you."

"This is not going to be easy," thought Rita. She was torn between accepting the flowers and crushing them into a wastebasket for William to see when he got home. Time after time during the day, she changed her mind about whether she could or would ask William to leave. Without him, she would have to live on her baby-sitting money, which amounted to about $180 per week. She had no idea how long it would take to go to court to arrange for William to pay child support.

That afternoon, when the children were asleep, Rita called several lawyers listed in the yellow pages of the phone book. They said they could take her case to court fairly quickly but that she would be required to ask for a legal separation. They'd be glad to take her case, but she'd have to pay $500 or more in advance.

As Rita talked, she became more and more frightened by the expense and difficulty of getting rid of William. He controlled the family's money. It would take Rita months to smuggle away $500 without his noticing. How many times would he beat her in those months?

William went crazy any time she showed any sense of independence. When she'd talked to him about getting a job outside their home, he'd thrown a fit and stormed out of the house, not coming back for more than a day. She'd been afraid to bring up the subject again. If he discovered that she had been holding out money from baby-sitting, she didn't know what he'd do. She imagined him trying to kill her.

Late in the afternoon, Rita got a telephone call from Shirley. "What are you going to do?" Shirley asked.

"I don't know. . . . I'm trying to figure out how to get him out."

"Honey, if you want him out and you have trouble, you gotta have a plan. Let's do this . . . if you think you might need help, you just call me here at the Candy Hut. When you hang up, I'll call the cops. I'll tell them that there's a hell of a fight going on at your place, and they'd better get over there right away."

"Oh God, Mama, what if we call the cops, and they don't take him away? You know what he'll do to me!"

"If you call, I'll take off from here. I'll be right over. If the cops don't get him out, then you could come home with me."

"Mama . . . I don't know if I should do it."

For a change, William was home on time. He noticed that Rita had carefully placed the roses in a vase on the dining room table.

"Where's my boy Sam?" he asked.

"Out back with the kids from downstairs," Rita replied.

"How about going out for supper?" he asked.

"Just you and me," Rita said with a smile.

"Uh huh," he replied with a grin.

William went into the kitchen, asking Rita if she wanted a drink.

"Let's not drink tonight," she said softly.

"I'm going to," he replied.

"No, let's not. It'll be nicer if you don't."

William continued to make himself a drink. Not knowing what to do, Rita went to the bathroom to get away and to have time to think. She returned to face William, still confused about what to do. She saw that he'd made a huge drink for himself.

"I'll call Mama to see if she can take care of Sam," Rita said.

Her hands shook as she tried to dial the number of the Candy Hut. Shirley answered at the other end.

"Mama . . ." said Rita.

"They're on their way," said Shirley, hanging up the phone before Rita could say another word.

Rita stood by the telephone, not knowing what to do next. Her mind was blank. Finally she moved. Going to the dining room table, she picked up the vase of roses.

Though she was now shaking all over, she carried the vase into the kitchen where William was. Seeing the roses, he smiled.

Rita carefully removed the roses from the vase.

"What are you doing?" he asked. She then placed the long stems in the garbage disposer and turned on the switch. First all the stems grew shorter, and then, one by one, the roses disappeared into the drain.

"Forty-five bucks," screamed William. "You're grinding up forty-five bucks, you stupid . . ."

Rita ran into the living room.

"What in the hell's the matter with you?" William shouted from the kitchen. He had not followed, and Rita suspected he was now drinking right out of the vodka bottle.

"You're going to have to get out!" Rita shouted. "Find another place because you can't stay with me, not even one more night!"

William came around the corner and into the living room, ready to fight. "I apologized!" he yelled. "Nobody's going to treat me this way!"

"Your apologies won't work. They're as phony as you are. Now get out!" Rita pointed at the door.

"Not me," shouted William. "You. You're on the way out." He grabbed and violently twisted her arm. Rita tried to pull away, and her sudden movement caused them both to fall.

For a brief time Rita was on top. All too soon, however, William again had her arm twisted behind her back and was pulling her hair. Rita swung with her other arm, but as she did, William pulled out some of her hair. From then on all Rita could do was to shield herself from William's blows. Then she lost consciousness.

He did not stop hitting her until after the police arrived. When Rita became conscious, William had been handcuffed and was being held on the sofa by a large policeman. His female partner tended to Rita.

"You OK?" the woman officer asked.

"Just a family squabble," Rita heard William say.

"I think he was going to kill me this time."

"Can you move your arms and legs?" the officer asked.

Rita moved her limbs. "Not broken," she sighed. She was having trouble catching her breath. "He can't stay here anymore . . . get him out . . . for good . . . please," Rita pleaded.

"Are you willing to press charges?" the officer asked.

"Yes . . . if that's what it takes."

Shirley arrived. "Oh God," she gasped. "How bad are you, baby?"

"Mama. Make sure they press charges."

"I'm calling an ambulance," the policewoman said. "But before it arrives I think we'd better talk. What you're going through is really hard, and most women have trouble trying to do it alone. There's a place where you can get help—a shelter for battered women."

"I don't know."

"I'll follow your case. When you get released from the hospital, I think it would be best to give them a try. They can help you with your feelings and with the courts, and if you're having trouble making it on your own, they provide a lot of help and support."

"OK," said Rita. "But for now, you make sure he doesn't come back here."

With help from a counselor from the Agency for Battered Women, Rita found the courage to press charges. In court, the judge ruled that William could not set foot in Rita's apartment again. Nor was he ever to touch her or to threaten her verbally or in writing. If he broke any of the court orders, he would be arrested and would serve a six-month sentence for the assault on Rita.

Rita also got help from a lawyer who was a public defender. At a second hearing, she got a legal separation. William was ordered to pay $35 per week in child support. As she left the courtroom, Rita was on the verge of crying. In the hallway, she saw William standing by himself. She turned in the opposite direction and began to walk away from him, but he ran up to her from behind.

"Neither of us wants this," he said.

"Don't," she replied, and her eyes filled with tears.

"We can start over. I'll stop drinking."

"I've loved the man. Shouldn't I give him another chance?" Rita asked herself.

"No," she said to William. "I'm starting over, but not with you."

"You'll regret this. You'll never make it without me," he said, walking away.

SCENE 6
Djuan

As usual, Djuan was awake before the alarm clock rang. He glanced at the clock and saw that it was 2:55 A.M. Turning off the alarm, he patted Yulanda and sat for a moment on the edge of the bed. Then he began to dress quietly. Carlo stirred in his cradle but did not wake up.

Djuan cooked a small breakfast, mixing vegetables and an egg, and in a corner of the pan he warmed rice. This morning he ate his meal right out of the pan. He checked on Tessa and Marissa before starting for work.

Work was a thirty-minute drive away, and it was still dark when Djuan entered the plant. He walked through the foundry's large casting room. The room had a dirt floor, and Djuan stayed on the well-packed trails around the edge. In the center, large molds with metal castings were cooling in the dirt. Those castings would be his work for tomorrow.

As Djuan entered the grinding room, he pulled the cord that turned on the lights above the work area. Today he was to grind the edgings off large discs that would be used to make street signs. One hundred of the discs were piled against the wall, a few feet from the grinding bench. Djuan's pay was based on the number of pieces that he finished. He would earn 57¢ per piece, and he guessed that he could finish ten of the signs each hour.

He quickly went to work, lifting a disc and slowly turning it around in front of the bench grinder. Then he set the piece on the bench, where it could be buffed with a hand tool.

After an hour, Djuan's back began to hurt, but in three years on this job he'd learned that the pain would go away if he kept working. By 6:00 A.M. he'd completed twenty-three pieces, but he would slow down as the day wore on. He figured he could finish the signs by 3:00 or 4:00 in the afternoon.

After another hour, Djuan heard someone enter the plant and approach his work area. It was the plant foreman, who as usual was the second worker to arrive for the day shift. "Morning, Djuan," he called, ". . . you're off to a good start."

"Morning," replied Djuan, stopping for a moment. "How many castings are there going to be for tomorrow?"

The foreman looked out toward the casting room and then back to Djuan. He was silent for a moment but then replied. "Not enough," he said sadly. "Turn off that machine and come talk." As the two men walked slowly toward the foreman's office, Djuan realized that something was wrong.

"You've been one of my best workers," the foreman said, "and it hurts like hell to have to tell you this. . . . The company was sold to a larger corporation, and they're shutting down this part of the operation. They say they'll make more money by closing us down than by keeping going."

"How can that be?"

"Taxes. If they close us, they save on taxes. It's bad news for both of us. I've been in the foundry business for thirty years, and with all the other closings I don't know what I'll do."

Djuan lowered his eyes and stared at the floor. "Let this be a bad dream," he thought. Silently he began to pray for the future of his children and his young wife.

For a time, both men said nothing. Finally the foreman walked to the door of his office and stood looking out at the remaining castings. "It stinks," he said quietly. "You and I have done our best . . . but when those castings are done, we're done."

Djuan returned to his bench in pain. Since he had been in the United States, this was the only job he'd had that paid enough to support his family. How could he tell them that he had no work? And what job could he find in a city that was full of younger men looking for work?

"We'll be OK," Marissa had once said. "You are strong. You will find work." But Marissa didn't know what it meant to be older, to have been born outside the country, and not to have gone to high school.

The next day, when the last casting had been buffed, the foreman suggested that Djuan and he go together to the Job Service Office to arrange for unemployment compensation. "I don't know," Djuan replied. "I want to work. I don't take money if I have not earned it."

"You have the money coming," said the foreman. "Part of what you earned over the last three years went to the government. Now every week they will give some of it back. When you find another job, you can begin to give them money again."

Djuan was to receive $150 per week, but the benefits would end after twenty-six weeks. "We cannot live for very long on the money," he told Yulanda. "Our rent is $300 a month. We will have food, but we cannot have the telephone or new clothes until I find work."

Yulanda turned her face sharply away from Djuan. Looking at the back of her head, Djuan sensed that something was wrong. "What is it?" he asked.

"What if we need a doctor?" she asked.

"We pay," he said softly.

Yulanda got up quickly and ran into the bathroom, slamming the door. Djuan heard her put on the lock.

Djuan got up and rapped lightly on the door. "You OK?" he asked. Yulanda was quiet. "What is it?" he tried. After what seemed like a long time, Djuan heard Yulanda move and the lock click again. As Djuan opened the door, Yulanda began to sob. He led her to the bedroom. "Tell me," he said.

"I am to have a baby," she said through her tears. "It is not a good time."

Djuan moved close to her on the bed, holding her from behind. Slowly he stroked her stomach. "I must find work," he said. "I will apply every day until I have a job."

Questions About the Story
MAIN IDEAS AND DETAILS

EXERCISE 11: Main Ideas and Supporting Evidence

Give evidence for or complete the following main ideas by filling in information from the story.

1. It will be hard for Rita to leave William because

    a.

    b.

2. William becomes very angry at Rita because

3. We know that Djuan is a good worker because

4. If Djuan completes one hundred discs, his pay for the day will be

    $$\underline{\hspace{2cm}} \times \underline{\hspace{2cm}} = \underline{\hspace{3cm}}$$
    pay for the day

5. Djuan loses his job because

    a.

    b.

6. It will be hard for Djuan to get another job because

    a.

    b.

    c.

EXERCISE 12: Matching

Match the details in the left column with those on the right by putting the letter of the correct answer in the blank.

____	1.	Djuan	a.	$500
____	2.	7:00 A.M.	b.	Djuan gets up
____	3.	unemployment compensation	c.	what William calls their fight
____	4.	William	d.	has worked in a foundry for three years
____	5.	3:00 A.M.	e.	unable to control his anger
____	6.	Djuan's rent on the trailer	f.	$180 per week
____	7.	child support payments	g.	the foreman comes to work
____	8.	the foreman	h.	$35 per week
____	9.	advance fee for a lawyer	i.	$150 per week
____	10.	Rita's weekly earnings from baby-sitting	j.	has worked in a foundry for thirty years
____	11.	family squabble	k.	$300 per month

EXERCISE 13: Recalling the Story in Your Own Words

Write a short answer of one to three sentences for each of the following questions about the story.

1. Why does William send Rita flowers and a necklace?

2. How does William respond when Rita shows signs of independence? Include an example from the story in your answer.

3. What is Shirley's plan to get Rita out of the house if Rita is having any trouble?

4. Why does Rita call Shirley at the Candy Hut?

5. What does the court order William not to do?

6. Tell where Djuan works and what he does.

7. The foreman says that Djuan has earned unemployment compensation. What reason does the foreman give?

ANSWERS ARE ON PAGE 177.

CHAPTER 3
Learning Independence

SCENE 1
Bob and Carol

Bob was trying to explain to Paul what was happening in his relationship with Carol. It was hard to explain because he didn't really understand it himself.
"She was like a really good friend," he said, ". . . not like some of the others I've messed around with. In fact, I didn't want to get really involved with her because I was afraid it would screw up the friendship."

"You're getting weird," said Paul.

"Maybe I am. But it worked out pretty well. It was like she couldn't stand just being friends, and I was playing hard to get. The more I hung back the more she seemed to want to get close. . . ."

"Well, that's different. Some chicks need to feel like they trust you. Then you can make your move."

"No. I don't really want to get into it, but it was more complicated than that. She was getting to be a good friend, and I really was afraid it would mess up a good thing."

Carol had wondered, too, what Bob was up to. After they'd seen each other four or five times, she was sure that Bob was as attracted to her as she was to him. But they were always doing something. They had very few moments when they were really alone. Finally she invited Bob to come over to her apartment for dinner, but he gave an excuse why he couldn't. "But let's go out a little later," he said. They went out to a spot that had live music. Carol waited patiently for Bob to ask her to dance.

For the first time with Bob, she began to feel hurt and angry. His not coming to dinner felt like a rejection. The feeling grew when Bob did not ask her to dance. Carol did her best to act charming, but as the evening wore on she found it hard to talk. She wondered if this would be her last date with him.

When they arrived back at Carol's apartment, Carol thought that Bob would expect to walk her inside to her door. He was in the habit of doing that. They would stand by her door for ten or fifteen minutes, making embarrassed small talk and deciding when they would see each other next. Earlier Carol had thought that tonight she would invite Bob inside, but that idea had grown stale. She was not in the mood to risk the possibility that he would make up another excuse. She'd had enough rejections for one day.

Bob stopped the car in front of Carol's apartment. He reached for the door handle as if he were going to get out. "Wait," said Carol, sliding over the seat in his direction. She grabbed the collar of his coat with her left hand and almost violently pulled his head around to face her. Then she grabbed the other side of his collar with her right hand. She looked him directly in the face for a moment. Pulling hard on his coat collar, she directed his mouth to hers and kissed him so hard that their teeth touched.

This surprised even Carol. She had thought about what she was doing but had no intention that their first kiss be like this. She sensed that Bob too was shocked by her assertiveness and by the force of the kiss. She softened her hold on him and pulled her head back. Then she kissed him once more, this time softly but only for an instant.

"Wow," said Bob, moving his head back so that he could see Carol clearly.

"I can let myself in tonight," said Carol as she stepped out of the car.

"Just a minute," he said, starting to get out of the car. "When will I see you again?"

"Anytime you want. You know that," she said, waving him back into the car. She turned toward him once more before she disappeared into her apartment. Her smile told Bob that she, at least for tonight, was playing hard to get. "It's a game that two can play," he thought. But suddenly it occurred to him that he'd already been playing the game for weeks. Now, in less than a minute, Carol had totally turned the game around on him.

As he drove toward home, he wondered what Carol was thinking. Remembering what she had said about his seeing her whenever he wanted, he decided to call her as soon as he got home. "But why wait till I get home?" he thought. He pulled his car into an all-night gas station and went to a telephone.

"Hello, Carol. Bob. You said I could see you whenever I want. I'll be right over." He hung up the phone without giving Carol a chance to say a word. As he drove up to the front of Carol's apartment, he saw that the lights were on. She let him in with a silly grin on her face. "If you think you're going to get dinner now, it's a little late," she said.

As weeks and then months passed, Carol and Bob became serious about each other. Though they had moved out of their parents' houses, their new relationship had unexpected effects on how they got along with their parents.

At first Bob hadn't even wanted Carol to meet his father. "You wouldn't like him," he said. "He really is a nasty old man." But Carol asked if she could spend part of Christmas Day with Bob and his dad. It would be the first time that Bob had spent any time at all with the old man since he'd moved out. Bob and Carol had gone together to get a tree and put it up in Bob's apartment. They invited his father over for a small Christmas supper. Not only was the old man friendly, he also clearly liked Carol, and she quickly became fond of him.

"It's nice to have a woman around again," the old man finally said. "Why don't you find someone like her for me? Even if the one you found were just a tad older, I wouldn't complain." The old man still had nothing good to say about Bob. But by showing that he liked Carol, he seemed also to be saying that he had forgiven Bob.

By spring, Bob was feeling comfortable with his father. He knew that Carol's being around helped them get along. The three had even spent a full day together trout fishing. Carol had suggested that they go fishing, and Bob and the old man had agreed. Bob and his father had fished a lot before Bob was in high school. This was their first outing together in years.

The day began before sunup as the three headed for the creek. Carol felt clumsy in the wading boots that they'd borrowed from a friend of Bob's dad. The day ended back at the old man's house. Carol insisted on frying the fish with the heads on "like trout are supposed to be fried."

"Not bad for a beginner, huh?" said Carol, as she showed Bob's dad the platter of eight trout. She'd caught five and the old man had only caught one.

"Not bad," said Bob's father.

Excitement was shining in Carol's eyes.

"I haven't played with worms since I was a kid," she said.

"It's cheatin' if you don't use flies," said the old man with a wrinkled grin.

"Maybe you don't want seconds then. You just eat the little one you caught on a fly."

"Forget it. Once they're fried and on the table, I don't care how they're caught. Not a bad job of cookin', Carol. You'd make Bob a fine wife."

Carol could feel the blush creep into her face and cheeks. She and Bob had never talked about marriage. She certainly didn't want such talk to go on here.

"I'll have to find a husband who can catch more than two trout in a day," said Carol, as she poked Bob under the table.

SCENE 2
Liz

Liz was impressed with how quickly things had happened once she had decided to attend the University. While her parents had not strongly encouraged her to go, they'd made it clear that they thought she'd made the right decision. Her mother immediately began to tell friends and relatives. She also talked to Liz about going on a shopping spree to buy the clothes she'd need.

Liz found that she had no desire to go shopping. She made one excuse after another for not going. When the excuses began to wear thin, her mother asked her point-blank if she wanted to go shopping at all. Liz told her probably not, but that she didn't know exactly why. That was the truth; she didn't know why except that she had a vague feeling that she didn't want to spend a lot of money on things she might not use.

Another seemingly small problem began to gnaw at Liz. As soon as people found out that she was going to college, they thought they had every right to ask her a hundred questions about her plans. "What are you going to major in?" seemed to be their favorite question. To Liz, the question seemed to be people's way of asking what she wanted to be when she grew up.

Liz soon realized that she had no idea what she wanted to be. That frightened her because everybody seemed to expect that she'd know by now. But it certainly didn't pay to tell people honestly that she didn't know. Then they'd just begin a new round of questions. "Well, what are you interested in?" "What courses did you enjoy most in high school?" Adults seemed to think she needed counseling because she hadn't fully planned the rest of her life.

But then it suddenly became clear to Liz why she hadn't gone shopping with her mother. She didn't know what she wanted to be, so she didn't know what she wanted to wear. What kinds of friends, if any, would she find at the University? What would they be like? What would they wear? Her mind raced over the possibilities. Suddenly she felt the full weight of not knowing where she was going or even very much about who she was.

During her solo experience on the mountain in Oregon, this problem seemed to have been solved. There she had felt a new spirit and commitment. But spirit and commitment were not things you could hold in your hand or even tell other people about. They were just thoughts and ideas that could only take shape when a person actually accomplished something. The problem was figuring out exactly what to do.

Liz had thought to herself about how clear and simple things seemed when she was alone on the mountain. She had become confused so quickly when she came down. She suddenly realized that she had felt most alive when she was totally alone.

As she thought about her future, she began to imagine reliving the mountain-top experience. She fantasized about becoming a poet or a painter. She would live alone, high enough and at a great enough distance from others that her view of the world would be a panoramic landscape. Her view would be so distant that she would never have to focus on details.

"But what about other people?" she asked herself. There was not even one other person in her fantasy. The thought that she really wanted to be alone was frightening.

"How can I find meaning and purpose if I'm isolated from other people?" she wondered. "I've got to find some way to get involved with other people . . . a job that has some importance for other people and for me."

But in the meantime, all Liz could do was to make the best of each day. Perhaps the pieces of her life would eventually fall into place in a way that made sense. Deciding on the smaller pieces was easier than thinking about the whole pattern at once.

In Oregon, Liz had gotten into excellent physical condition. Staying in shape, she thought, would be one of the pieces. Each day for the rest of the summer, Liz either rode her bike or jogged. Usually she jogged to the University campus, three miles from her parents' house. There was a path that ran for almost a mile and a half next to the lake; it was a favorite spot for Liz and for many joggers.

Liz stopped to see Shirley at the Candy Hut at the end of one of her long bike rides. It was a hot August day, and high school was out for the summer. The Hut looked smaller and more run down than she'd remembered it. The only other customer was some jock who'd been in her graduating class. He was sitting in a back booth reading a magazine.

"Hi there," said Shirley. "Long time no see."

"H'lo, Shirley. How you doin'?"

"Not much goin' on, girl. I'm just keepin' the place clean and waitin' for mothers to bring their kids in for ice cream. Not many your age around in the summer, you know. They're all at the beach. 'Cept that one there." She pointed to the jock at the back of the Hut. "He's been stoppin' on his way to work. I guess he's always on second shift."

"Have you seen any of the old crowd?" asked Liz. "You know, I was gone for a lot of the summer, and I've kind of lost track of people."

"Oh, a few been in and out. You know I have trouble keepin' track, but I think you're one of the only ones that graduated."

"That's just about right, Shirley. Most of them just didn't make it."

"Say, you know, girl, you always did stand out from the crowd. What are you going to do now?"

"I thought I'd have a root beer float."

"Well, that's not exactly what I meant. I was askin' what you'd be doin' in the fall."

"I know that, Shirley," said Liz with a smile. "I'm just tired of trying to answer that question. . . . Actually, I'm going to the University, but I have no idea what I'm going to be."

"That's OK, girl. Hell, you're just startin' out. I never went to college, but I'm smart enough to know that most people figure out what they're gonna be while they're there, not before they go. How're you supposed to know before you tried some things? I bet you'll stand out there just like you did here."

"Well, I don't know about that," said Liz. "I guess I'll just figure things out a little at a time. But I know I'm not going to find out much about where I'm going by just studying and going to class. I did that already in high school. I want to get involved in doing something for other people."

"I always figured you were one who had her head on straight. I probably shouldn't be givin' you advice, but I got one idea for you. . . . I know someone who was gettin' beat up by her old man, and she went to the Agency for Battered Women and got help. I hear that place don't pay all the people who work there, but it's somethin' you could do that would get you some experience. . . . I think you might be real good at workin' with people."

"Maybe," said Liz. "That's the kind of thing I had in mind."

"I figured," said Shirley. "You're movin' out of your old crowd. You just might like workin' with people who got troubles. God knows it's important. . . ."

When Liz left the Candy Hut, the jock in the back booth came to the counter. "Who was that girl?" he asked.

"Who wants to know?" asked Shirley.

"My name is Ted Schmelzer," said Ted. "I think I graduated with her, but I don't even know her name."

"Well, we never did go much by names around here," said Shirley.

"She's really a knockout," said Ted. "I wonder why she was never a cheerleader or prom queen."

"You'd have to ask her."

"But I can't do that if I don't know her name."

"I'll tell you what, if I ever start a dating service, I'll let you know. Then we'll see if ol' Shirley can fix you up."

Questions About the Story
MAIN IDEAS AND DETAILS

EXERCISE 1: Identifying Main Ideas

Circle the letter of the choice that best completes each sentence.

1. When he is first dating Carol, Bob is slow to get involved because
   a. he really doesn't care for her much
   b. Paul tells him to take it easy
   c. he doesn't want to risk losing her
   d. Carol is playing hard to get

2. Carol feels hurt and angry because
   a. her parents don't want her to date Bob
   b. Paul seems to have no respect for her
   c. Bob doesn't understand her problems at work
   d. Bob won't come for dinner or dance with her

3. Though Bob has been playing hard to get, everything changes when
   a. Bob decides to come back to Carol's apartment
   b. Carol kisses him and ducks into her apartment
   c. Bob and Carol dance close
   d. they have a late dinner together at Carol's

4. Bob's father first shows that things are OK between him and Bob by
   a. showing how much he likes Carol
   b. taking Bob and Carol fishing
   c. calling Bob and inviting him for Christmas
   d. sharing all the fish he caught

5. Liz does not want to go shopping for school clothes because
    a. her mother always tells her what to buy
    b. Liz feels she already has enough clothes
    c. her mother always chooses the wrong stores
    d. Liz doesn't know what she will be doing

6. Liz is frightened by her own thoughts about the future because
    a. she finds being alone very appealing
    b. she isn't sure she can succeed at the University
    c. she wants to be with John, but he's a thousand miles away
    d. painters and poets don't make very much money

7. In Liz's conversation with Shirley, Shirley suggests that Liz should
    a. begin dating Ted, the jock at the Candy Hut
    b. decide on a career before starting college
    c. try working at the Agency for Battered Women
    d. help her start a dating service

EXERCISE 2: Sequence

Put the following events in the order they occurred in the lives of the characters. The first event should be number 1.

____   a. Bob and Carol went out to hear music.

____   b. Bob, Carol, and Bob's father went fishing.

____   c. Bob came back to Carol's apartment.

____   d. Bob, Carol, and Bob's father had trout for dinner.

____   e. Bob gave an excuse for not coming to dinner.

____   f. Carol kissed Bob.

____   g. Bob, Carol, and Bob's father had Christmas dinner.

VOCABULARY

EXERCISE 3: Matching

> A **synonym** is a word or phrase that means the same or almost the same as another word or phrase. For example, a synonym for *under* is *beneath*.

Match each underlined word or phrase on the left with its synonym from the column on the right by writing the correct letter in the blank. Then write a sentence of your own using the matched word. The first one is done for you as an example.

_f_   **1.** He was <u>in the habit of</u> doing that.
I am accustomed to hearing my husband sing in the shower.

a. fantasized
b. bother
c. gorgeous
d. came to like
e. broad
f. accustomed
g. forwardness
h. apart
i. wish

_____   **2.** Bob was shocked by her <u>assertiveness</u>.

_____   **3.** She quickly <u>became fond of</u> him.

_____   **4.** She had no <u>desire</u> to go shopping.

_____   **5.** A problem began to <u>gnaw at</u> Liz.

_____   **6.** Her view would be a <u>panoramic</u> landscape.

_____   **7.** I'm <u>isolated</u> from other people.

_____   **8.** "She really is <u>a knockout</u>," said Ted.

_____   **9.** She <u>daydreamed</u> about becoming a poet or a painter.

APPLICATION

EXERCISE 4: Relating to Your Own Life

Write down your thoughts about each of the following questions in a paragraph of four to six sentences. If possible, discuss your answers with others in your class.

1. Traditionally, our society has expected men to take the lead in relationships between men and women. Carol is quite assertive in her relationship with Bob. Do you think her assertiveness is attractive or unattractive? Do you feel that men should take the lead in relationships? Why or why not?

2. In this chapter, Liz is confused about what she wants to do for a living. List what you feel are three important considerations in deciding what kind of work you want to do. Explain why each is important.

EXERCISE 5: Scenes in Your Life

Write a short essay of about three paragraphs on the following topic. If you can, discuss the topic with others before you write. Don't worry too much about grammar. Think through your ideas carefully, and write so that others will understand what you have to say.

Liz and Shirley talk easily with each other, and they seem to have a lot of respect for each other. Liz is about eighteen, and Shirley is in her sixties. What might they offer each other?

Consider your own life. Identify two relationships you have with people whose ages are very different from yours. What value or insights have you received from your relationship with each? How could you enrich your relationships with these people?

ANSWERS ARE ON PAGE 177.

SCENE 3
Ted

Ted was beginning to feel very successful in his work. The company had asked him to stay on full-time. And the tasks that he was asked to do were important and required a lot of responsibility. In addition, the people were good to work with because they recognized Ted's interest and abilities.

When Ted began to work full-time, he also began to form close friendships with other workers. This also meant that others shared company gossip with him. Much of this gossip centered around Mr. McKenna, who owned the company. Everybody seemed to be trying to figure out what kind of man they all worked for. Ted had to admit that Mr. McKenna was an interesting subject.

Ted had seen and met Mr. McKenna several times, but, like the rest of the workers, he didn't know quite what to think of him. "The boss," as they called him, didn't spend much time at the office. But when he did come in, he'd sweep through the plant talking to everyone he saw. Mainly he asked questions. It didn't seem to matter if someone was the print boy or the head of the design department because the boss seemed equally interested in everyone.

His unannounced visits were a cause of concern because nobody wanted to appear to be doing a bad job. The workers never seemed to know when or where he'd turn up. Stories about what the boss had done had become legends within the company. Several times he'd shown up on construction sites driving a battered company truck and wearing blue jeans and a hard hat. Once he'd stayed all day to work with the carpenters.

But in contrast to that story, there was another episode. The Vice President of the United States had come to town to campaign. The boss had brought him over to the plant without telling anyone that they'd be coming. As they'd toured the plant, Mr. McKenna introduced the Vice President to the workers by name and asked many of them to explain exactly what they did.

Another time the boss had discovered that there was a problem on a construction site 1,500 miles from the main office and that it looked like the job wouldn't get done on time. It was a Friday afternoon. Everybody else was ready to do nothing about it until the following week, but Mr. McKenna wouldn't hear of that. He called the airport to get the company plane gassed up. He got together eight of the company's best carpenters and electricians and told them to go home and get their toothbrushes because they'd be working out of town over the weekend. "I know it's a burden, and you'll have to cancel some plans," he said. "But there'll be an extra week's pay for everybody and a $500 bonus if we get caught up."

"Who's gonna buy the beer?" one of the carpenters asked.

"And I'll buy the beer," said the boss with a smile.

So the stories about Mr. McKenna pointed to his being a man of action who was not at all afraid of getting his own hands dirty. He was also very impressive in a business suit and was comfortable with people like the Vice President. The more Ted heard about the boss and saw him in action, the more intrigued he became. He wanted to understand how anybody could command so much power and respect.

Then, late one night, Mr. McKenna stepped into the computer room just as Ted was finishing the last of a day's work. "And what did you do today, Schmelzer?" he asked.

"I did the materials takeoff for the job that's coming up in Canton, Ohio."

"What's the bottom line for materials on Canton?"

"It looks like $2,200,000," answered Ted nervously.

"How many square feet are we putting in down there?"

"Just a minute, I'll ask the machine. . . . Here it is, about 49,000."

"So what's the cost per square foot on Canton?"

"Well, I'll see what the computer says. . . . Looks like we'll run close to $45 per square foot."

"How old are you?" asked Mr. McKenna.

"Eighteen," replied Ted, wondering anxiously why he was getting so much attention.

"Are you going to school, or do you just work for me?"

"Right now I'm just working. I graduated from high school last June."

"Well, you seem like a bright young man. Have you thought about going on in school?"

"I've thought a lot about it, sir, but to tell you the truth, I like working here."

"We're glad to have you. But let me tell you something about this business. There are 100 other companies out there trying to do what we do. We're successful, and most of them are not. The reason is that we've been able to keep ahead of the pack by constantly changing and improving. If we sit back and coast even for a couple of months, part of that pack is going to catch us. So I always hope that my people will keep looking for ways to learn. This computer setup is good, but it's going to be up to people like you to tell me how I can make it better."

"I see your point," said Ted.

"Is there ever going to be a better time?" asked the boss. Without waiting for Ted to reply, he continued. "Why don't you register at the University or at the Technical College? Pick up a few courses. I'll leave a note in the business office telling them to pay your tuition. We'll pay you like we normally would even though you're going to slip away to attend classes."

"Sounds like an offer I can't refuse."

"I'd be disappointed if you did. Let me know how it's going."

Ted felt as if he were in a daze as he walked across the parking lot to his car.

"The boss must think I'm good," he thought, "or he wouldn't invest the money in me. But at the same time he's really challenging me to be better." Ted didn't know whether to feel hurt because he hadn't set high enough goals for himself or just feel good about having the company pay his way to school.

"What a dumb thought," he said to himself. "What good would it do to feel hurt?"

Then his thoughts turned to the episode in the Candy Hut. He'd made a mental note to himself to look through his yearbook to find the name of the beautiful creature he'd seen talking to Shirley.

When he got home, he walked directly to the bookshelf to get the yearbook. Opening it to the pictures of graduating seniors, he began with the As and started looking at all the faces of his class. "There she is," he thought. "But she doesn't look half as good in a picture as she does in real life."

"Oh God, don't tell me," he said out loud. "It can't be true."

Beneath the picture was the name *Elizabeth McKenna*.

SCENE 4
Paul

Paul's landlord sat quietly in an empty room just down the hall from Paul's. He was listening attentively and had gone to the window when Annie had left for work. Now he was hoping that Paul would leave too. Another one of his renters had complained that Paul's stereo was keeping him awake late into the night. He'd also mentioned that people often came and went from the apartment throughout the night.

"I'd better have a look at the place," the landlord thought. He did not see himself as nosy. However, he had to protect the reputation of his property and the rights of the other tenants. From the beginning he hadn't been too sure about Paul. Paul had seemed too young, and he'd also been vague about where he worked. Something smelled fishy, and the landlord wanted to put his mind at ease.

At eleven o'clock he heard Paul's stereo go on. Just before noon it went off, and a door opened. From behind the drapes, the landlord saw Paul leave the building. The landlord brought some tools with him so that if he were caught red-handed in Paul's apartment, he could always claim to be working on the building's heating system.

Once inside Paul's apartment, he began making mental notes of the problems. He knew immediately that he wanted Paul out of his building and that he'd begin eviction proceedings. But it was worse than that. Paul appeared to be a thief. When he'd seen enough, he called the police.

"I've discovered a theft," he said. "Can you send someone over?"

He met the policeman as he came up the front steps. "You've had something stolen?" the policeman asked.

"Well, not exactly. Nothing was taken from me. . . . But it looks like one of my tenants has a little theft ring going."

"I see. What makes you think the tenant is a thief?"

"Come with me and see for yourself. The guy's room is full of cassette decks and stereo equipment. . . . Here we are. Just look in here."

"Wait a minute," said the cop. "I don't go into someone's apartment without a search warrant." He stood at the doorway and watched as the landlord moved through the apartment, pointing out evidence of Paul's criminal activities.

"You're right," said the cop. "This guy's dealing in stolen goods, but I don't know if I can help you. I'm not coming in there. It's against regulations unless you've got a warrant. You can come down to the station and file a complaint, but you better have a good reason for knowing what's in the guy's apartment. Otherwise the case will never get to court."

"Come on. You gotta be kidding," said the landlord. "I show you this stuff, and we both know it's stolen. You're telling me you're not gonna do a thing about it?"

"That's not exactly what I said. In a case like this, we have to obtain evidence in a legal way. Landlords can't just let themselves and cops into people's apartments to look around. The law doesn't allow it. Now that doesn't mean we can't nail this guy. But it does mean that we're not going to nail him this afternoon. You'll just have to give us a little time. For now, give me the name and description of the guy who lives here."

That afternoon, Paul's name was run through the police computer. When the computer turned up no information, a search of juvenile records was also made. "Yeah, we have him in here," the clerk said. "His name has popped up here ten or twelve times in the past couple of years . . . suspected of burglary, suspected of drug sales, missing from his parents' home, truant from school, juvenile drinking. But he's still a minor. . . . Let's see . . . he'll turn eighteen in about three weeks, on the twenty-fourth of February. You want Juvenile to take the case?"

"Maybe not. Three weeks isn't a long time to wait. Let me talk to the Detective Bureau and get back to you."

By the next morning, Paul was under surveillance. The police planned to spend the next three weeks building a case against him. They would spring the trap sometime after his eighteenth birthday.

Questions About the Story
MAIN IDEAS AND DETAILS
EXERCISE 6: Summarizing Main Ideas

> To **summarize** means to pick out only the essential information. When you summarize, you want to get the point across in as few words as possible.

Complete the following by summarizing events and ideas from the reading. One is done for you. Use a separate sheet of paper.

1. Stories circulate about Mr. McKenna, Ted's boss. Write a summary of each of the three stories in one to three sentences.

   Story 1: *He would sometimes come to a construction site and help the carpenters.*

   Story 2:

   Story 3:

2. These stories say a lot about Mr. McKenna. Following the stories, the main ideas about Mr. McKenna are summarized in a few sentences. In your own words, summarize what we know about Ted's boss.

3. Summarize the reasons why Paul's landlord sneaks into Paul's room.

4. Summarize the reasons why the policeman would not enter Paul's apartment.

5. Summarize the reasons why the landlord would want Paul evicted.

EXERCISE 7: Recalling Details in Your Own Words

Answer the following questions in your own words in one or two sentences. Each question asks you to recall an important detail from the story.

1. Mr. McKenna gives Ted a reason why his company is successful and others are not. What is the reason?

2. When Mr. McKenna says that he'll pay Ted's way to the University or Technical College, Ted has mixed feelings. What are they?

3. When the landlord goes into Paul's apartment, he takes tools with him. Why?

4. What evidence of criminal activity does the landlord find in Paul's apartment?

5. What plan do the police make for dealing with Paul?

READING BETWEEN THE LINES
EXERCISE 8: Making Inferences About the Characters

> When you make an **inference**, you discover an idea that is implied but not directly stated.

Complete the following by making inferences about the characters.

1. List three qualities that Mr. McKenna would like in an employee.

    a.

    b.

    c.

2. Why is Ted so shocked when he learns the name of the beautiful girl he saw at the Candy Hut?

3. The landlord breaks the law when he enters Paul's apartment without telling Paul in advance. Does the landlord know that he is breaking the law?

    a. List at least one piece of evidence from the story suggesting that the landlord *does* know he is breaking the law.

b. List at least one piece of evidence from the story suggesting that the landlord *does not* know that he is breaking the law.

APPLICATION

EXERCISE 9: Privacy and Protection

To figure out what another person's **point of view** might be, look at the situation through that person's eyes.

Answer the following questions in a few sentences. Think carefully about your answers. If possible, discuss the questions with your classmates. Use a separate sheet of paper.

Paul's landlord enters Paul's apartment without permission. The landlord feels that he has good reason to suspect that Paul is damaging the apartment or that he is using the apartment for criminal activity.

Answer questions 1 and 2 from the point of view of Paul, the landlord, and other tenants living in the building.

1. Should the landlord have a right to search the apartment? Why or why not?

   a. From Paul's point of view:

   b. From the landlord's point of view:

   c. From the point of view of other tenants living in the building:

2. Should the police have the right to search the apartment? Why or why not?

   a. From Paul's point of view:

   b. From the landlord's point of view:

   c. From the point of view of other tenants living in the building:

3. Does the law requiring a search warrant adequately protect the rights of Paul, the landlord, and other tenants? Explain.

ANSWERS ARE ON PAGES 177-78.

SCENE 5
Rita

"When's Daddy coming home?" Sam asked for the third time.

"Your daddy isn't going to come back here," Rita answered. "But we'll arrange for you to go see him sometime."

"Doesn't Daddy like us?"

"He'd like to come home, Sam, but he can't live here anymore."

"He's strong and a good fighter. I saw him fight. Will I grow up to be like Daddy?"

"In some ways," Rita said, but to herself she thought, "God forbid."

"You can be strong like your dad . . . but don't fight," she continued. "Police are even stronger than your dad, and they stop fights. Maybe you'll be a policeman when you grow up."

Rita did not know what to do about Sam. He seemed to worship his father, and it troubled Rita to think that he might be trying to grow up to be like William. And William had visitation rights. Whenever he spent time with Sam, the boy seemed to come home all the more like his father.

At least William always brought Sam back. At first, Rita had dreaded the visits because she worried that William would kidnap or just try to keep Sam. William had contributed to her fear by threatening to sue her for custody of Sam. Because she was already having a hard time making ends meet, Rita knew that she would not be able to afford a lawyer for a custody battle. She wondered if a public defender would take a custody case. She also worried that a public defender might not do an adequate job of defending her right to have Sam.

As the weeks went by, Rita was aware that her moods changed constantly. Some days she felt thrilled with her independence. But too soon she'd begin to feel sad, lonely, and afraid.

She shared these feelings with Shirley. "God, I hope we didn't make a mistake," Shirley replied. Because of the comment and the look on Shirley's face, Rita knew that Shirley was beginning to blame herself for Rita's problems.

"It's OK, Mama," Rita said. "There are more good times than bad. We did what had to be done, and I'm going to be fine." But as Rita spoke, she decided that she could not tell Shirley about some of her problems. It wouldn't be fair to make Shirley feel bad too.

Her moods continued to swing from high to low. Rita felt that she would explode unless she could talk to someone about Sam, about money problems, and about what she was going to do with the rest of her life.

She remembered that the Agency for Battered Women had offered to provide counseling and support. "Counseling?" she had thought. "Why counseling? It's not me that's crazy, it's William." Later, however, it occurred to Rita that maybe what they had in mind was just talk. The talks they had had about going to court to get a separation had certainly been helpful. Nobody had treated her as if she were crazy then.

On the following Saturday, William took Sam, and Rita took the bus to the agency. She entered and approached the receptionist's desk.

"Hi," said the receptionist. "Can I help you?"

"I don't know," said Rita. "I was here a couple of months ago when I had husband trouble, and I'm afraid I'm not doing so well."

"Tell me more," she said, ". . . and we'll see if we can help. By the way, my name's Liz McKenna."

Rita began to tell Liz about her problems and her need to talk. "It's not an emergency, then?" Liz asked.

"No," said Rita.

"I'm not a counselor," Liz said. "I'm in the training program learning to be a counselor, and I watch the desk on Saturday mornings. If you have an emergency, I should call in someone with more experience. If not, we can talk. I don't have much else to do except answer the phone. . . . Let me get you a cup of coffee."

Rita sat down, accepting the coffee. "I do want to talk," she said. "I was here several months ago and got separated from a bad marriage, but I'm having problems. . . ." Liz nodded and continued to listen, only interrupting to ask Rita to explain things she did not understand.

When Rita had told her story, she stopped. Almost an hour had gone by. "I've taken so much of your time," she said to Liz.

"That's what I'm here for," was Liz's reply.

"I feel better. You seem to understand the problem, and for some reason that's a help. What do you think? Do I need counseling?" asked Rita.

"What we just did was counseling," Liz replied.

"That's counseling?"

"That's what we do here. You're in control of the situation. We just try to understand your point of view and help you find a direction." Both women laughed.

"You're a good listener," said Rita. "Now how about helping me find some direction?"

"While you were talking, I was thinking about a few things you might do. You're looking down the road into the future. You're concerned about both making more money and finding a job that's more satisfying than child care. Have you ever considered getting your high school diploma and maybe getting more training? I'm sure you could do it."

"What kind of job would I do?" Rita asked.

"I don't know . . . but there are vocational counselors at the community college. They could help you find out what you're interested in and what you're good at. The college also has a GED program where you can get a high school equivalency diploma, even if you've been out of school for a long time."

"I have to get going on something," Rita said. "I will check with the college. Can I call you to tell you how it went?"

"Sure. Or better yet, come back next Saturday and we'll talk again. I took this job because I wanted to get experience working with people. If you don't come back, I'll just be sitting alone waiting for the phone to ring."

As Rita got up to leave, she started to shake hands with Liz but changed her mind. Instead, she held out both arms and gave Liz a hug. "I'm glad you were here," she said. "I feel better because of our talk. . . . See you next week."

SCENE 6
Djuan

Tessa and Marissa were old enough to understand how hard it would be for the family if Djuan could not find work. Though Djuan and Yulanda had tried to hide their fears, the girls were very aware of their sadness and worry about the future.

"Will we have to move back to a housing project?" Marissa had asked.

"I don't think so," Djuan said. "I am strong and a good worker. I will find something." But in the weeks that followed, Djuan's last paycheck and most of the family's savings were used up. Djuan read the help-wanted ads of the newspaper each day and applied for many available jobs.

Occasionally he found work that lasted for a few days, setting up displays in department stores or working as a laborer on a short-term landscaping project. When he found work, he'd return home with food for the family rather than with money. "We must eat," he told Marissa. "Yulanda must eat for herself and the baby. You must eat so that you can do your schoolwork."

But the few jobs that Djuan found were not enough. At the end of each month, the family had only rice and canned vegetables to eat, and there was no milk. Then one day Tessa came home rather late. She was carrying two bags of groceries containing milk and chicken and fresh fruits and vegetables. "Where did you get the food?" Djuan asked.

"It is not important where I got it," Tessa replied. "There will be more. We will not be hungry."

"Tessa," Djuan scolded. "You cannot get food without money. Where did you get money?"

"I work, Papa. I work to help buy food. I take care of children, and I am paid $10 a day."

"But Tessa, you cannot work and go to school."

"I am not going to school," she replied. "Instead I work."

Djuan glared at Tessa. "I will work, and we will have food," he said.

"It is not your fault," Tessa said. "I know you want to work, but if I can help, I must. I will go back to school when you find a job."

"We need the food, and I should feel lucky to have a daughter who cares so much about her family. But you must finish school. You must tell them that you can't work anymore because of school."

"Papa, I thought about Yulanda when I saw a card on the bulletin board that said there was a job. I thought Yulanda could take care of the children. But I know how you feel about that. . . ."

Djuan was beginning to get angry. "It is not your business," he said.

"I didn't ask, Papa. I didn't interfere, I just thought . . ."

"It is my job to feed the family. It is Yulanda's job to keep the house and raise children."

"Papa, you came to America to start a new life. But you hang onto a custom from before. In America women work like men, and their husbands are not hurt or ashamed."

Djuan was ready to end the conversation with his daughter. "I do not care about custom," he exploded. "Your mama worked. . . . Who do you think you are? What makes you talk like this to your father? You know what happened to your mama." Then his eyes filled with tears. Tessa approached Djuan, but he turned away from her. She put both arms around his waist from behind. "We're going to be all right, Papa," she said.

"I don't know," he said. After a moment he spoke again. "I want you to be happy. To get a good job, you need to go to school. For Yulanda it is different. Her time for learning is gone. She is a mother and is having another child."

"You want Marissa and me to have good jobs and to be like American women, but you don't want the same for Yulanda. Caring for children is safe. . . . Yulanda is only ten years older than me, and she is good at caring for children."

"I will talk with her. Maybe she could care for Carlo and also for others. But Tessa, your job is to finish school. I will make sure there is food on the table."

On the following day, Tessa, Yulanda, Carlo, and Djuan went to the home where Tessa had been caring for children.

"My daughter must go to school," Djuan explained, ". . . but my wife can care for your children."

That evening, when Yulanda and Carlo returned, Yulanda placed a ten-dollar bill on the kitchen table. "It is not very much," she said, ". . . but it will buy milk. I think I like working."

Djuan hugged Yulanda. "It was hard for me," he said. "I don't like sending you off to work, especially when I have no job."

"It is OK," Yulanda replied. "It is the American way, and I am American."

Tessa, however, had not been content to just return to school. She'd continued to look for a part-time job that she could do before or after school. Within a few days, she came home with an application form for Djuan to sign.

"There is a newspaper route available," she announced. "It is a morning route that will pay about $30 a week. I will be done delivering by six-thirty each morning, and I will be in school by eight o'clock."

The paper route became an early morning project for Tessa and also Marissa, who had not wanted to be left out as a contributing member of the family. And Djuan was unable to lie in bed while his daughters were out working, so he too helped out.

The money from the paper route and Yulanda's job and the unemployment compensation and food stamps that Djuan received were all placed in a cigar box. The box was hidden behind the towels in the hall closet. Although everybody except Carlo put money into the box, only Djuan took money out. "It is very hard for him not to have a job," Yulanda told Tessa and Marissa, "so he will be in charge of how the money is used."

Questions About the Story
MAIN IDEAS AND DETAILS

EXERCISE 10: Main Ideas and Supporting Evidence

The sentences in this exercise summarize some of the main ideas from the chapter. List at least one piece of evidence from your reading that supports each main idea.

1. Rita is afraid that Sam will become like his father.

   Evidence:

2. Rita fears that she will have trouble keeping Sam.

   Evidence:

3. Rita is concerned about her own mental health.

   Evidence:

4. Going for counseling seems to have a positive effect on Rita.

   Evidence:

5. Tessa and Marissa are willing to work hard to help the family.

   Evidence:

6. Djuan is determined to get a job.

   Evidence:

7. Djuan wants his daughters to finish school.

   Evidence:

EXERCISE 11: True or False

Indicate whether the following statements are true or false by putting a *T* or an *F* in the blank.

_____   1. Sam is impressed by his father's fighting.

_____   2. Sam understands why his father left home.

_____   3. Once William is gone, Rita's worries about what he will do are over.

_____   4. Rita decides that she shouldn't talk openly to her mother about her problems.

_____   5. After her divorce, Rita has more bad times than good times.

_____ **6.**   At first, Rita does not feel that she needs counseling.

_____ **7.**   Counseling does not help Rita.

_____ **8.**   Djuan and Yulanda cannot hide their problems from their children.

_____ **9.**   Djuan is able to make sure that his children always have milk to drink.

_____ **10.**   When Yulanda does go to work, she resents Djuan's being able to stay home all day.

_____ **11.**   At first, Djuan does not want Yulanda to work.

_____ **12.**   Yulanda does not like working.

VOCABULARY

EXERCISE 12: Synonyms

Each sentence in this exercise contains an underlined word. One of the choices that follow is a synonym for the underlined word. Circle the letter of the correct synonym. Then write a sentence using the underlined word *in the original sentence*. The first one is done for you as an example.

1.   We'll arrange for you to see him.

   a.   intend

   (b.) plan

   c.   meet

   Tina can easily arrange a dinner for 100.

2.   Heaven forbid.

   a.   help

   b.   willing

   c.   prevent

   _____

3.   Rita worried about their doing an adequate job.

   a.   poor

   b.   satisfactory

   c.   bad

   _____

4. Rita <u>dreaded</u> the visits.

    a. feared

    b. sought

    c. needed

5. William threatened to sue her for <u>custody</u> of Sam.

    a. guardianship

    b. janitorial

    c. child support

6. There are <u>vocational</u> counselors at the college.

    a. religious

    b. employment

    c. recreational

7. You hang onto a <u>custom</u> from before.

    a. law

    b. design

    c. tradition

8. I didn't <u>interfere</u>.

    a. butt in

    b. demonstrate

    c. leave

APPLICATION

EXERCISE 13: The Characters' Beliefs

People's feelings and actions are often determined by their **beliefs**. For example, Bob believed that his father was a nasty old man. This belief determined his actions and feelings toward his father for a long time. However, as you know from reading the story, he is eventually able to become comfortable with his father.

Sometimes the characters in the story act just the way you would expect them to, based on their beliefs. In other cases, they act in ways that contradict their beliefs.

Answer the following questions about the characters' beliefs.

1. Bob believes that he should move slowly in establishing his relationship with Carol.
   a. Give one example of an action Bob takes based on this belief.

   b. Give one example of an action that he takes that contradicts this belief.

2. Paul believes that because he is a minor, he cannot get in serious trouble with the police.
   a. What actions does he take based on this belief?

   b. How could his belief get him in trouble?

3. Rita has believed that she does not need counseling.
   a. Why does she change her mind?

   b. Does she benefit from her counseling? How?

4. Djuan believes that his role in the family is to work, Yulanda's is to take care of their home and children, and Tessa's and Marissa's is to go to school.
   a. What does Tessa do that contradicts Djuan's beliefs?

   b. What major change happens in Yulanda's role as a result?

   c. Does Djuan change his belief about Yulanda's role?

   d. Does Djuan change his belief about Tessa and Marissa's role?

ANSWERS ARE ON PAGES 178-79.

CHAPTER 4
Problems and Decisions

SCENE 1
Bob and Carol

Things changed very quickly for Bob and Carol. Though they had never talked about marriage, their lives were flowing in that direction and they both realized it. Both Carol and Bob were saving money so that if and when they were married, they could get off to a good start.

Carol's job at the supermarket allowed her to save some money each month, and she actually enjoyed the work. However, she felt a sense of conflict about continuing. The image of being on a treadmill still popped into her mind. In contrast, Carol imagined that Millie's daughter, the emergency room nurse, must have a totally different feeling about her work.

"But why would I want that kind of responsibility?" she asked herself. "Why would I want another person's life to depend on my skill?" At the supermarket, people counted their change. If she'd made a mistake, it was easily corrected. But in an emergency room, it would be a different story. There, mistakes could have a permanent effect. The thought was frightening. At the same time, however, Carol thought about Millie's pride in her daughter and about the challenge of a job like nursing.

There was one other aspect of becoming a nurse that stood in the way. She'd have to go to school for at least two years. She'd heard from friends that the two-year programs at the Technical College were really not so bad. The friends who went to "Tech" related that they were in classes with adults of all ages. It was very different from high school. At Tech a student came and went as he or she pleased and was treated like an adult. The work was harder, they said, and some of her friends had been shocked by the amount of homework. But they all seemed confident that it was going to be worth the effort. Graduates of Technical College programs almost always found good jobs in their field of training.

Carol had once thought that she had nothing to lose by going to Tech. But that was before she had begun to think about marriage. How could she save any money if she were a full-time nursing student? At best, she could only work half-time if she went to school full-time. She could hardly live on half-time pay, much less put money aside.

She shared these thoughts with Bob. "You can move in with me, and I'll pay the rent," he said. "Maybe two can live as cheaply as one."

"Do you mean it?" she asked.

"Sure," he said. "You'd just have to do your share of work . . . the cooking, the cleaning, the laundry, the shopping, and taking out the garbage." He grinned.

"What's left that would be your share of the work?"

"I give up," he said. "What's left?"

"Nothing," she replied, "and that would make me hard to live with."

"Oh, geez, this sounds like blackmail."

"Well, not exactly. If I went to school full-time, and worked part-time, and did all the housework, I'd be a bear. . . ."

"We could give it a try. You do as much as you can, and the minute you start feeling like a bear, I'll take over."

"Bob, I feel like growling just from thinking about it. The housework would have to be fifty-fifty. . . . You know, the other problem is my parents. They'd go bananas if I moved in with you. I think they already suspect that you've been staying at my place."

"What's the problem? Why don't they just treat you like an adult?"

"They've always been strict about that kind of thing. I think they have a really hard time letting go."

"What if we were engaged?"

"If we were engaged, we would have talked about marriage and made some definite plans," she said with a sly smile.

"I mean, what would your parents think about our living together if we were engaged?"

"I couldn't even think clearly about that unless we really were engaged," she said, laughing out loud.

"I think I'm being had," said Bob. "You're leading me on and I'm following like a little puppy. . . . The thing that really worries me is that I love it. . . . Let's say we're engaged."

"You mean it?"

"Yeah," he said. "I mean it."

"Are we really engaged then?" Carol asked.

"I think so," he said. "But it feels like there ought to be some papers to sign or something."

"Normal people give the woman a ring," she said. Carol's eyes filled with tears.

"Are you OK?" Bob asked.

"Oh, I've never been better," she said, kissing him.

After a while Bob said, "The way you led me on, I'm surprised you didn't already have a ring handy."

"Maybe we can find something."

"How about the pop top to a beer can?" asked Bob with a laugh. He went to the refrigerator and pulled the top off a can. He dramatically got down on his knees to put the ring on Carol's finger.

"You see what I mean," she giggled. "You really aren't normal." They laughed together and lay in silence for a moment on the couch. Carol brought her left hand up to admire the ring, and they began to laugh again. After a while Bob said, "I think this all started when I asked what your parents would say about our living together if we were engaged."

"And I couldn't think about it because we weren't engaged," she said. "But we are engaged now, right?"

"Yeah. That ring means we're engaged."

"OK then, let me think. What would my parents say about us living together if we were engaged. . . ?" Carol began to giggle again. "They still wouldn't like us to live together," she said. Now she was giggling uncontrollably. Bob pushed her off the couch and onto the floor. He sat on her stomach and held both her hands so that she couldn't move.

"You mean it doesn't make any difference?" he asked.

"Not really," she said laughing. "They think you can't live together unless you're married . . . period."

"But you knew that all along."

"Maybe I did and maybe I didn't. Do you still feel like you've been had?"

"I guess so . . . but like I said, I love it. Where are you going to live? Here or at your place?"

"Here. There's nobody to push around over at my place. But I'll have to get out of my lease."

"What are you going to tell your parents?"

"Someday they'll find out, and I guess we'll just go from there."

But even before Carol moved in with Bob, trouble began to brew with Carol's parents. They discovered that Bob had been staying overnight at Carol's apartment. This discovery took place a little bit at a time. First, when Carol's parents called, Bob sometimes answered the phone. Also Carol's mother questioned her about having men's clothes in her closet and shaving equipment in the bathroom.

"Bob stops by after work sometimes without going home first," Carol explained.

"He might as well move right in. He seems to have everything he needs right here!" said her mother. "I don't know if your having your own place is really a good idea."

Carol let the conversation die, but that was not the end of the matter. Several weeks later, Carol's mother dropped in unexpectedly on a Saturday morning. She found Bob and Carol in their bathrobes.

Carol's mother said almost nothing at the time, but the features on her face became rigid. Her mouth froze in a kind of half smile. Without moving her lips she hissed, "I'd better not stay." Later that day Carol's father called and asked that she come over so they could have a talk. When Carol arrived, her father was in a rage. Within a few minutes, it became obvious to Carol that he wouldn't listen to a thing she said. It seemed to Carol that her point of view and her feelings meant nothing to her parents. It appeared, in fact, that they were about to disown her.

"Nobody's going to call any daughter of mine a tramp."

"But Daddy, sleeping with Bob does not make me a tramp. How could you possibly think I'm a tramp?"

"What do you call a girl who sleeps with men she's not married to?"

"But Dad . . ."

"And if you want to get married, I don't see how you expect to have a church wedding."

"He's a jerk," Carol thought. "And he's about to get me in a double bind. He won't be satisfied with anything less than a church wedding and now he's saying that I shouldn't have one."

Carol stormed out of her parents' house with tears streaming down her cheeks. Her mother, too, began to cry. Her father, however, seemed to have no sympathy for Carol. He continued to be angry and resentful.

Bob was at Carol's apartment when she returned, still crying.

"He's a total jerk," said Bob, "Who needs him?"

"But he's my father."

"I'd like to punch him out."

"Please, Bob."

"Who needs 'em," Bob repeated. "We've got $350 saved, and we can have our own wedding whenever we want one."

As the conversation continued, they decided to get married very soon. They would also try to regain her parents' goodwill. Somehow they would make their wedding a happy celebration, in spite of whatever her parents said or did.

A day later, Carol's mother called to invite the couple over for Sunday dinner.

"God, she's strange," Carol told Bob. "She called and acted as if nothing happened."

"Did you tell her to forget it?"

"No. I said we'd come."

Neither of them knew what they could or should say to Carol's parents. Deep inside, Bob felt like fighting with them, telling them to go straight to hell. Carol felt the same way but had not admitted it even to herself. She knew that such a scene would destroy whatever relationship with her parents she had left for a long time to come.

As Carol pushed open her parents' door, she felt Bob jab her lightly from behind, pushing her forward. "Here goes," he whispered. "Chin up!"

"Hi," said Carol.

"Hello," said her mother with her face frozen in a half smile.

"Good going," muttered her father, not even turning his head away from the ball game on TV.

Bob and Carol sat together at the extreme end of the couch feeling tense and isolated. Nobody talked.

Carol's father grunted to no one in particular as a Yankee scored from second base on a single.

"We're having pot roast," said Carol's mother after a while. "How've you been?"

"Good."

Carol's father moved forward in his chair as if he were going to get up, but he stopped abruptly, took off his shoes, and sat down again. Bob realized that he hadn't said anything since they'd come in. He wondered how long this scene would go on.

Finally Carol's father turned to her. "So what's with you?" he asked.

"I'm fine, if that's what you mean," she said.

"That's not exactly what I meant," he said.

"Bob and I are planning to get married," Carol blurted.

"La de da," said her father sarcastically. "Who are you going to get married to?" He couldn't hold a straight face and began to laugh at his own joke. Then he frowned again and looked at the TV.

"Sometime in June," said Carol, ignoring both her father's humor and his frown.

"Let's go," Bob whispered to her. But Carol stayed on the couch and put her hand on Bob's leg to prevent him from getting up.

"We're thinking about writing our own marriage ceremony," Carol said.

"Oh? Aren't you going to get married in a church?" her father asked.

"Well, yes. But these days people add their personal touch to the ceremony."

The conversation seemed to be making Carol's father even angrier. His face was flushed. "You can't get married in the church if you don't use the words of the Scripture," he shouted. "Where did we go wrong? People have been getting married this way for hundreds of years and now all of a sudden . . . Where did we go wrong? . . . You move downtown for a few months and come home with all these half-baked ideas like you're some kind of women's libber."

"Carol may have a point," said her mother.

There was complete silence as all eyes turned toward her.

"Weren't our wedding vows good enough for you?" shot back her father.

Bob and Carol suddenly found themselves watching the parents fight with each other. The argument peaked when Carol's mother suggested that they rewrite their own marriage vows and scratch "obedience."

Carol's father screamed back, "For twenty-five years you haven't obeyed me anyway, but I'll be damned if I'm going to put it in writing!" He stormed out of the room.

"The poor man's been under a lot of stress lately," whispered Carol's mother.

"But he's always been uptight about certain things. . . . There's one thing I haven't said yet. I'm going to move into Bob's apartment until we get married."

Carol's mother looked stunned. "Don't tell him now," she said. "I don't think he could take that." She got up and walked to the kitchen. After a moment, Carol followed and found her mother standing over the sink. Both her hands were placed firmly on the counter as if she needed them there for support. "You know we approve of Bob," she said. "But living with someone before you're married goes against everything we tried to teach you. We can never condone that!"

"I know," said Carol. They stood silently for a time, the mother looking out the window and her daughter behind her, able to see only her mother's back.

Finally Carol's mother spoke again. "You're a big girl," she said. "You seem to have decided what to do already. But don't you dare expect that your father or I will ever approve of it."

"But mother . . . I . . ."

"No. Let me finish. You know very well why we can't approve. As far as we're concerned, you're on your own. Maybe it would be best if you and Bob left us alone now."

"What about the wedding?"

"We'll see, Carol. We'll see."

SCENE 2
Paul

Paul had mixed feelings about turning eighteen. It meant that he could lease an apartment, buy a car, or get a loan in his own name, so he'd be even more independent. But at the same time, he thought about the burden of responsibility. It wasn't that his life would change so that he'd have to *be* more responsible. The problem was that he could be held responsible for anything he did.

Paul considered himself to be a smooth operator when it came to the police and the courts. He'd always been able to turn on a childlike charm that conned the socks off the police and social workers. He'd found out very early in life that adults were suckers for "children" who admitted their mistakes, showed remorse about what they'd done, and promised to lead a new life. "You've helped me understand that what I did was wrong" and "You've helped me to grow up" became two of his standard lines. Paul was smart enough to realize that this kind of talk worked because it flattered adults. It convinced them that they were doing a good job helping him.

Paul knew that being an adult changed the rules of the game completely because the police and the courts looked at adults very differently. Cops and judges would no longer feel obligated to "help a poor misguided child." Instead their jobs would be to protect society from adult criminals. That meant they would try to lock up a person for as long as possible. Paul had reason to worry.

He'd thought about going straight as soon as he turned eighteen, and he'd even tried working. His girlfriend Annie had helped him get some work as a dishwasher at the restaurant. Paul found this a grueling way to make a few bucks. After an eight-hour shift, he took home less than $30. Paul was used to making far more than that on one sale. It frustrated him to think that life would get worse instead of better when he became an adult.

Annie had a hard time understanding why Paul was so reluctant to take a real job. She felt that she was making enough money at the restaurant. She also looked forward to going to work because the people there had become her friends. Paul had not worked there enough to become a real part of the group, and Annie encouraged him to get more involved. When Paul would not, Annie was left with two groups of friends, those whom she worked with and others who were friends of Paul's.

Annie decided, however, to have a birthday party for Paul. She would invite her friends as well as Paul's friends. She was a bit anxious about this plan because she didn't know how well the two groups would mix. Some of Paul's friends were like Bob. They worked at real jobs and were almost as straight as her restaurant friends. But many of Paul's friends were more like Paul. They seemed to look down on people who led a fairly straight life.

In spite of her worry, Annie went ahead with her plans. She bought a full barrel of beer and expected forty people. It would mean "standing room only" in their small apartment.

The day of the party, Annie thoroughly cleaned the apartment. She moved the car stereos and other treasures of Paul's out to the back porch. Bob and Paul went to get the beer, and then Bob went to pick up Carol and bring her back to the party. They tapped the keg of beer, and soon the apartment was filled with people.

"I didn't know who you used to hang around with in high school," Carol said to Bob. She was referring to Paul and Paul's friends, who had moved to the back porch. The beer flowed, and the volume on the stereo got increasingly loud as the room filled with people. The front door was open, and the party spilled out into the hallway of the apartment building.

Annie mentioned to Carol that many of the people weren't invited. They were friends of friends who were invited. One hour into the party it looked like they'd need more beer. Bob started moving through the crowd to take up a collection for another barrel.

Suddenly there were rapid movements in the hallway. The word spread that the police were coming in. The hallway cleared and two policemen made their way to the front door. One of them knocked on the door, which was already open, and asked for Paul. "He's in the back," someone said. Bob hurried to the door. "Can I help you?" he asked the police.

"We want Paul Rafsky," one said.

"Paul's not here," said Bob.

"He lives here, doesn't he?" asked the cop.

"Yeah, he lives here, but he's not home right now," said Bob.

"Look, someone else just told us he was in the back. You better not be lyin' because we've got a warrant for his arrest. If you're lyin', we can get you for obstructing justice."

"Like I said, Paul's not here. Now why don't you look for him somewhere else."

People were starting to make their way to the front door of the apartment to leave. One policeman stood at the door. He let them out one at a time only after he was sure that each was not Paul. Annie stood helplessly behind Bob. Carol saw that she had started to cry.

The second policeman started to walk toward the kitchen and the back of the apartment, but Bob stood in his way. "Where are you going?" asked Bob.

"We know he's in here," said the cop. "We saw him come in with you and the beer."

"He can buy beer. He's eighteen," said Bob.

"That's why we're here," said the cop.

"Because he bought some beer?"

"No, Dumbo, because he's eighteen. Now get the hell out of my way so we can get this over with." He pushed Bob to one side. Bob stumbled and the crowd of people put him back on his feet. Pushing people aside, he started to reach for the policeman, but a hand came out of the crowd and grabbed him by the hair, jerking him back. Bob grabbed the hand that held his hair and wildly spun around. He came face to face with Carol.

"Don't you dare," she screamed. "You'll both end up in jail."

"The pig hit me," said Bob.

"Don't be a fool," said Carol. "He's got a warrant, and you're not going to stop him."

People filed out of the apartment one by one. Bob sat down in a chair as the apartment emptied. "Paul's had it," he thought. "He's on the back porch, and not only is it screened in, but also it's a long way to the ground."

But soon only Bob, Carol, Annie, and the two policemen were left in the apartment. There was no sign of Paul. "I don't know how he did it," Bob whispered to Annie.

"I wonder if I'll ever see him again," she said.

Questions About the Story
MAIN IDEAS AND DETAILS

EXERCISE 1: Identifying Main Ideas

Complete the following sentences. Each sentence should identify a main idea from the story.

1. Carol wonders whether she can afford to go into nurse's training because

2. Bob and Carol become engaged when

3. Carol's parents are upset with Carol because

4. Paul has mixed feelings about becoming an adult because

5. The police come to Paul's birthday party in order to

EXERCISE 2: Matching

Match the people or things in the left column with those in the right column by writing the correct letter in the blank.

_____	**1.** a nurse	**a.**	a friend of Carol's at work
_____	**2.** Carol's father	**b.**	the technical college
_____	**3.** Paul	**c.**	has a party for Paul
_____	**4.** engagement ring	**d.**	prevents Bob from getting arrested
_____	**5.** $350	**e.**	pop top from a beer can

____	**6.** Annie	**f.**	under a lot of stress lately
____	**7.** Tech	**g.**	a dishwasher's take-home pay for one day
____	**8.** Carol	**h.**	what the cop calls Bob
____	**9.** less than $30	**i.**	Millie's daughter
____	**10.** Dumbo	**j.**	Bob and Carol's savings
____	**11.** Millie	**k.**	cons the socks off the police

VOCABULARY

EXERCISE 3: Synonyms and Antonyms

A **synonym** means the same as another word, while an **antonym** means the opposite. For example, a synonym for *powerful* is *strong*. An antonym for *powerful* is *weak*.

Below you will find some phrases or restatements from the reading. For each underlined word, write a synonym and an antonym in the spaces provided. Then write two sentences of your own, one using the *original underlined word* and the other using *your antonym*. The first one is done for you as an example.

1. Bob and Carol were <u>tense</u>.

    synonym *uptight*   **antonym** *relaxed*

Bruno was tense as he entered the ring against Deadly Dick. However, he became relaxed after Dick went down on the first punch.

2. He stopped <u>abruptly</u>.

    synonym _____   **antonym** _____

3. . . . a <u>grueling</u> way to make money

    synonym _____   **antonym** _____

4. She was <u>anxious</u>.

    synonym _____   **antonym** _____

5. . . . <u>obstructing</u> justice

    synonym _____   **antonym** _____

6. Bob and Carol felt <u>isolated</u>.

synonym _____   **antonym** _____

7. . . . scratch the word "<u>obedience</u>"

synonym _____   **antonym** _____

APPLICATION

EXERCISE 4: Point of View and Personal Values

In this chapter, Carol's parents are very upset because Carol's mother finds Bob and Carol in their bathrobes in Carol's apartment on a Saturday morning. And when Carol tells her mother she is moving in with Bob before their wedding, her mother is even more disturbed.

Think about the following questions and write a few sentences in response to each. If possible, discuss your answers with your classmates. Use a separate sheet of paper.

1. Think about why Carol's parents might be so upset.

   a. What reasons might they give for objecting to Carol's plans?

   b. What values might their point of view be based on?

2. Now consider Bob and Carol's point of view.

   a. What reasons might they give for going ahead with their plans?

   b. What values might their point of view be based on?

3. Now consider your own point of view about unmarried people living together. Think of your own experience and of the experiences of people you know.

   a. If you could advise Bob and Carol, what would you tell them?

   b. What values of your own might your advice be based on?

   c. In what ways would your personal experience or knowledge of the experiences of others determine your advice?

   d. Do you think Bob and Carol should be free to make their own decision, regardless of your advice or Carol's parents' point of view? Why or why not?

ANSWERS ARE ON PAGES 179-80.

SCENE 3
Ted

Ted's classes at the University met on Tuesday and Thursday afternoons. He registered for Sociology 101 and for Principles of Accounting. Sociology met for an hour and fifteen minutes, accounting for a full two hours. He expected that he would like the accounting course better than sociology, but that was not the case.

The accounting professor required Ted and the other students to use a pencil, paper, and ledger sheets and to "show all their work." The first half of the two-hour class was always a lecture by the professor followed by a question and answer period. Then the class was asked to work on the homework assignment for the next class.

Ted objected strongly to having to spend an hour doing homework in class. He told the professor that he could do the work in a few minutes on the company's computer. There he could type all the entries and ask the machine to do whatever the textbook called for. He could even provide a typewritten printout. "That won't do," the professor said. "This course is designed to teach certain principles. If you're going to understand the principles, you've got to learn the whole process by hand."

"Oh, come on," Ted thought, "give me a break," but he said nothing more to the professor about it. There was a tremendous amount of homework required for the course. At times Ted did the assignments on the company computer and then copied the answers onto the ledger sheets.

"I just don't know why I'm doing all this," he thought. "Mr. McKenna pays for me to go to school because he wants me to help the company, but here I am learning how they did accounting twenty years ago." But down the hall from his accounting class, there was another room that contained computers like the ones at Ted's office. The thought of getting through the basic courses and moving to that room kept him going.

The sociology class was a different story. The class dealt with a person's relationship to society. The professor often drew the class into heated discussions. She'd provoke these discussions by arguing that people needed a strong government to guide their actions and behaviors. She claimed that, without the strong hand of government, life would be nothing more than "survival of the fittest." Most of the class seemed to disagree with her. The students argued strongly against the need for having a government to regulate their lives.

For the first time in his life Ted became a very active student. He was often class leader in arguing against the position taken by the sociology professor. But when the semester grades were reported, Ted got a C in sociology and an A in accounting. It was ironic, he thought, to get a C in a course that he liked so much and had put so much effort into and to get an A in a course that he hadn't really liked.

After his last class, Ted often drove back to work past the University gyms and the jogging path used by many students. Once he'd seen Elizabeth McKenna jogging on the path next to the road. He'd had the sudden impulse to slam on the brakes and leap out of the car. He would run alongside her for a moment and say something that would get her attention. He imagined trying to run up to her and having her think he was some kind of nut. . . . He'd end up chasing her down the path. Now that would be a hell of an introduction! "And even if I could catch her I wouldn't know what to say," he thought.

Each day as he drove back to work, he kept his eyes peeled for Liz. Every day he thought about what he might say if he had the chance to talk to her. Nothing he thought of seemed any good. He could be really direct and say, "I like your style." Or he could ask her a question about her running. Or he could ask if she was in his graduating class. He kept imagining that she would either ignore his statement or give him a very short answer. Then they'd stand and look at each other with nothing more to say.

But Ted had not seen Liz running for more than two months. He realized that he probably never would meet her. In fact, he began to think about her less often.

But then one day on his way back to work, Ted spotted Liz jogging on the path. His mind again raced over all the things he might say. He slowed the car as he approached her. He found himself wanting desperately to stop, but the foot that was on the car's accelerator seemed to have a mind of its own. The car passed Liz and continued down the road. Ted's eyes riveted on the rearview mirror as Liz's face came into view. He then turned halfway around in order to get a direct look at her face. Then he heard the bending of steel and the shattering of glass as the car hit a tree. Ted slipped into unconsciousness with the image of Liz's face in his mind.

SCENE 4
Liz

Liz knew that she was two miles from the gym because her watch indicated that she'd been running for fifteen minutes. It was an ordinary day of jogging until a car ahead of her went out of control. It crossed over onto the jogging path and hit a tree. She thought about screaming as the accident was happening, but later she could not recall if she'd actually screamed or just thought about it.

The left front fender of the car hit the tree first. The force of the accident pushed glass and steel into the space where the driver had been. Fortunately, the driver had been thrown to the right into the passenger seat. The impact had thrown open the door on the passenger side of the car. The injured man lay with his head hanging over the outside edge of the seat.

The car was engulfed in steam because the radiator had burst. As Liz approached the car, it reminded her of an old-time black-and-white horror film in which fog was used to create an eerie scene. The man was bleeding from his head. The vivid color of the blood contrasted sharply with the cloudy atmosphere created by the steam. The engine of the car was still running with a high whine, and the noise added to Liz's confusion about what to do. She looked over the top of the car to the left and the right, but there was nobody in sight.

She turned her attention to the man and fought off the sudden urge to panic and run. The first-aid training that she had received at the wilderness camp began to come back to her. "Check the breathing first and then the bleeding," she told herself out loud. She put her hand and then her ear to the man's mouth. She was reassured to find that he was breathing.

She thought about moving his head but decided against it because he might have a broken neck. Liz stooped down to get a better look at the cut. It was still bleeding hard. She considered trying to make a bandage but decided she could not tie it in place without moving his head. She had no choice but to put pressure on the cut with her hand to try to slow the bleeding.

She grasped the man's head with both hands. With her right hand she pushed her fingers against the cut behind and above the man's left ear. "God, I wish someone else was here," she thought. She could see a car a half mile down the road, but it turned into a parking lot. Liz shifted her weight, trying to find a comfortable position. It was difficult to apply pressure but keep from moving the man's head.

She looked at Ted's face. She had the feeling that she'd seen him before. He had probably been both handsome and athletic-looking. Now his face was an ashen white. He was twisted around in the seat so that it was hard to tell how tall he was. She checked his breathing again and found that he was doing OK. Another jogger came into view, moving slowly up the road. Liz figured it would be at least five minutes before he got there. She wondered if she shouldn't let go of the man and run as fast as she could to a telephone.

Another car came into view and moved slowly in her direction. It seemed to take forever to make its way to the scene. It stopped and a man got out hurriedly. "We need an ambulance right away," Liz said.

"Is there anything I can do?" the man said.

"Not unless you're a doctor."

"I'm not."

"Then maybe you can just get to a phone and call the rescue squad. I think the guy's doing OK, but it could be a serious injury."

The man sped off and the jogger approached. "Oh, God," said the jogger. "What happened? Is there anything I can do?"

"That other man went for help. . . . I'm just applying pressure to stop the bleeding."

Within a few minutes, the rescue squad arrived. A police car was not far behind. Ted was carefully placed on a stretcher for the ride to the hospital.

"Is he going to be all right?" Liz asked.

"I think so," the paramedic said. "His vital signs look good, but it's lucky for him that you stopped the bleeding. If he'd lost much more blood, he would have gone into shock."

"Where are you taking him?" she asked.

"St. John's," he said as they sped off.

Liz stood for a moment looking at the blood on her hands. Her body began to shake as she thought about what she'd just been through. The policeman offered her a ride home or back to the gym, but Liz said that she needed to be alone. She walked back to the gym where her street clothes were. It was a strange feeling to have devoted such thought and energy to helping the man and then to realize that she didn't even know his name.

The evening of the accident, Liz went to her parents' for dinner. When she got there, her father was just coming home from work. The two entered the house together. After they greeted her mother, Liz told her parents what had happened to

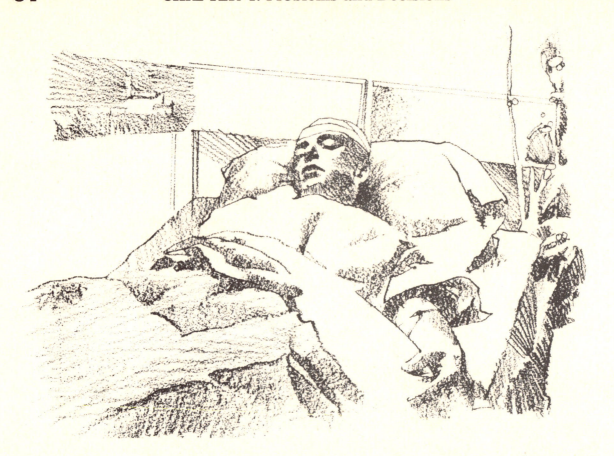

her that afternoon. She finished by saying, "So there I was, standing by this wrecked car with blood all over my hands. I might have saved the man's life. But I don't know what happened after they took him off to the hospital."

"This has to be more than a coincidence," said Mr. McKenna. "One of my employees was in a serious accident today. He'd gone to class at the University and didn't return. Finally his mother called to tell us he wouldn't be back—at least for a while. Kid's name is Ted Schmelzer and he's at St. John's. I'm going to see him tomorrow. You're welcome to come along if you're interested in knowing if he's the man. You might as well try to find out the ending to your story."

"So it sounds like he's going to be OK. Is that what his mother said?"

"She didn't really know. He wasn't conscious yet."

The next day Liz followed her father and a nurse toward Ted's room. "He was conscious this morning, but he's been asleep most of the day. His mother has been with him the whole time," the nurse said. Mr. McKenna introduced himself and Liz to Ted's mother. "I work with Ted," he said.

Liz looked toward the sleeping man. He'd gotten some color back in his face. Liz was shocked to see that they'd shaved most of the hair off his head.

"How's he doing?" Liz asked.

"He seems to be OK," said Ted's mother. "When he was awake, he knew me and was talking. The doctor said that there was no sign of anything being wrong inside his head."

They talked for a short time, mainly about Ted's work. After a short while Liz looked again at Ted. She discovered that his eyes were wide open and he was looking directly at her.

"I think he's awake," said Liz.

"Are you OK?" Ted's mother asked him.

Ted continued to look at Liz. Finally he spoke. "I must be dreaming," he said.

"You're doing fine," said his mother. "You're in the hospital."

"It must have been a dream," he said. "Or else I'm in heaven."

"I think you're disoriented," said his mother. "Maybe I better call a doctor."

"Aren't there two people right there?" he asked.

"These are friends of yours, Ted. Liz McKenna and Mr. McKenna from your company."

"Oh God," said Ted.

"Maybe he's had enough visitors for today," said Mr. McKenna. "I'll stop back after he's had a couple more days rest."

"Me too," said Liz. "See you later."

"Really?" asked Ted.

"Yes, in a couple days," said Liz.

"Oh, I wonder if he's OK," said Ted's mother. "He doesn't seem to be making any sense."

Questions About the Story
MAIN IDEAS AND DETAILS

EXERCISE 5: Recalling Important Details

Complete the following in a few sentences. Use a separate sheet of paper.

1. Describe Ted's behavior in each of his University classes:

    a. accounting

    b. sociology

2. Why does Ted have an accident?

3. Briefly describe the accident, giving at least five details.

4. When Liz arrives at the scene of Ted's accident, she has to think quickly about what to do.

    a. List two actions that she considers taking but does not.

    b. List two actions that she does take to help Ted.

5. To everybody in the hospital room, Ted appears to be disoriented or confused. List at least two things he says that sound irrational.

EXERCISE 6: Sequence

Put the following events in sequence by numbering them in the order that they occurred in the lives of the characters.

____ **a.** Mr. McKenna heard about the accident.

____ **b.** Liz decided not to move Ted's head.

____ **c.** Ted's accident occurred.

____ **d.** Liz went to her parents' house for supper.

____ **e.** A man in an auto stopped at the accident scene.

____ **f.** Ted began classes at the University.

____ **g.** Ted did his homework on the company computer.

____ **h.** Ted talked to Liz for the first time.

APPLICATION
EXERCISE 7: Issues Raised by the Story

Ted has strong feelings about his two University classes. This exercise requires that you examine the issues that Ted faces. Complete the following on a separate sheet of paper.

1. Ted's accounting professor feels that to understand the principles of accounting, students need to do work by hand and not on a computer. Ted feels that the professor's ideas are old-fashioned. Apply this question to your own education by answering the following question about learning basic math.

   a. Imagine that you are taking a basic math course. What advantages would there be to you if you completed the assigned work without a calculator?

   b. If you used a calculator in the course, what advantages to you would there be? List two.

   c. Considering both sets of advantages, would you prefer to use a calculator or to work by hand to learn math? Explain your position.

2. In his sociology class, Ted's professor argues that a strong government is necessary to guide people's actions. Ted argues against the professor's position. The following questions require you to consider both sides of this issue.

   a. List three ways in which government protects you from harm. List the way the government is involved (for example, "law against theft"), and the protection it provides ("protects my property").

Government Involvement	Protection
(1)	(1)
(2)	(2)
(3)	(3)

b. List three situations in which you think the government is too involved in our lives. Explain your answer and tell what the consequences would be if the government were less involved.

(1) situation:

why government is too involved:

consequences if government were less involved:

(2) situation:

why government is too involved:

consequences if government were less involved:

(3) situation:

why government is too involved:

consequences if government were less involved:

ANSWERS ARE ON PAGE 180.

SCENE 5
Rita

"Mama, I think I'm going to be OK," Rita told Shirley. "I don't know what you'll think of this, but I've been seeing a counselor. I think it's helping. . . . You know how hard things were for a while."

"A counselor, huh?"

"I went back to that agency that helped me with the separation. I've been talking to a counselor on Saturdays. . . a woman a little younger than me named Liz."

Shirley dropped the coffee cup that she was holding, and it smashed as it hit the floor.

"You OK, Mama?"

"Yeah. I'll get the broom." Shirley swept up the broken cup. "I'm glad you're doin' better," she said. "You know how I get worried."

"You're not going to believe this, Mama, but I think I'm going to get a high school diploma. I took some practice tests, and I passed three out of five. I've got to study some, but I didn't do that bad. They tell me I'll pass the next time."

"Not bad, girl. I always knew you were no dummy. What're you gonna do when you're a high school graduate?"

"I've been thinking about that too. They gave me some tests to take that are supposed to tell what you're good at and what you're interested in. They tell me I'm a people person. But I'm also an outdoor type. I might not like a desk job. I got a computer printout with jobs that I might like. It had things on it like being a forest ranger."

"A forest ranger?" Shirley smiled. "You'd be wearin' one of those big hats with the flat rim and carryin' a little shovel?"

Now Rita smiled. "You mean Smokey the Bear," she said. "To be a forest ranger, most people go to college for four years. I can't do that. But you know, I've been thinking about something else. They think I might like being a cop."

Shirley dropped another coffee cup, and it smashed as it hit the edge of the counter.

"Geez! You're full of surprises," she laughed. "We better stop talkin' or I'll be completely out of dishes . . . a cop, eh?"

"What do you think?"

"Well, you don't see many lady cops. But I sure liked having a woman there when they came to get William. If you think that's what you want, more power to you, baby."

Rita had developed a sense of where she wanted to go. Passing the GED gave her further confidence and hope. Through the counselor at the community college, she learned that the police department was seeking applicants for the police academy, a twenty-week training program for future officers.

It will be a rough twenty weeks," he cautioned. "But if police work is what you want to do, you might as well have a go at it."

The career side of Rita's life was, however, only half the story. Her personal life didn't progress at the same rate. It was lonely and embarrassing for Rita to be single again after eight years of marriage. She dreaded the idea of going to a restaurant for dinner by herself. But she knew she'd have to learn because there were weekends when Sam was with William and she was totally alone and bored.

When she finally got up the courage to go out to dinner, she entered the restaurant, indicated that she was a party of one, and was seated by the hostess. Immediately she was overwhelmed with the feeling that everyone in the restaurant had noticed that she was alone. She was sure they were talking about her. For a few minutes, she sipped a glass of wine, feeling very uncomfortable. She wished that she had brought a book or magazine to read so that she wouldn't have to watch people whom she suspected were watching her.

Starting to panic, she told the waitress that she wasn't ready to order. When the waitress returned, Rita asked for the check for the wine, saying that she wasn't feeling well. She stared at the plate in front of her for what seemed like an eternity until the waitress came back. Her face and ears burned as she got up to pay her bill and leave.

Rita was also concerned about how well she was doing raising Sam. Getting her GED had taken a lot of effort. She had often studied late into the night.

Trying to make a living, be a mother, and be a student all at once, Rita felt that she was pulled in at least three directions. And she often felt tired and impatient when Sam demanded her attention.

William had bought Sam a Big Wheel, a three-wheeled bike, which he constantly wanted to ride in the parking lot of a nearby shopping center. Because he was too young to be trusted to ride on his own, he demanded that Rita take him. For more hours than she wanted to count, Rita paced the pavement at a corner of the shopping center. Sam sped around, laughing and talking to her, even when she was too tired to answer him.

Rita often had second thoughts about leaving William—or at least about being single. Her personal life as a young single woman was not turning out as she had hoped.

She could share her successes and her frustrations with Liz, Shirley, and some of the women from the neighborhood. And she cherished her independence. But she could not seem to shake the lingering thought that her life should somehow be tied to a man.

"Are you going to start dating?" Liz had asked her.

"I think I'd like to," she said, ". . . but I don't know if I have enough energy left to give to a relationship."

SCENE 6
Djuan

As the months passed, Djuan found it hard not to become bitter. He'd been a hard-working and honest employee since he'd come to America. And he would work very hard again for any employer who would hire him. But the city had many industries closing, a high rate of unemployment, and many applicants for every available job. He knew what a good worker he would be, but he could not seem to communicate his ability in a job interview. Trying and failing to find jobs had begun to hurt.

One of Djuan's friends who was also unemployed had turned to crime in order to live better. He would pick up forged credit cards and purchase goods from stores. The same man who gave him the credit cards would buy the radios, televisions, and toasters that were purchased with the phony cards. Then every week Djuan's friend would get a new card so that he wouldn't be caught.

He'd tried to convince Djuan that it was a foolproof scheme and there was no chance of going to jail. Djuan had been tempted, but in the end he could not go through with it. It wasn't that he feared getting caught. It was just that he could not be part of a dishonest scheme.

As spring approached, Djuan realized that his six months of unemployment compensation would soon be over. He would still not have a steady job. "We're going to have to pick fruit and vegetables this summer," he told the family.

"We can't," said Marissa. "We lost Mama because we were picking."

"You hush," Djuan said. "Don't you bring up your mama."

"OK. But Papa, we worked so hard to get where we are. How can we go back to picking?"

"There is no other work for me," he said. "And my unemployment is almost gone. We picked before and we can pick again." Djuan sounded certain about his decision as he spoke to Yulanda and his children. But he could not sleep at night. The decision to pick was frightening. They would make money, but he'd lost his first wife while picking.

When it was time to leave, the family stored most of its belongings in the basement at the home of Djuan's cousin. The cousin would try to rent the trailer to someone else for the summer, but he'd expect them back in the fall. Yulanda cried as they left the city.

"I don't like this any more than you do," Djuan snapped. Then he and the entire family were silent for a long time.

Finally Yulanda spoke. "I am a good picker," she said. "I will carry your baby and pick. You will be proud . . . and Marissa will watch Carlo. But at the end of summer I will be too fat. Then you must promise that we go back home to have the baby."

"We'll do that. You are a fine woman and I am already proud. You will do some picking, but I will do enough for both of us. And Tessa will work and so will Marissa when you are watching Carlo."

Late that night, they pulled into a rest area next to the highway. As they passed a streetlight, Djuan noticed that the car was making a cloud of smoke from the exhaust pipe.

"Engine trouble," he thought. But he did not tell the others.

They ate sandwiches and then slept in the car. In the middle of the night, Yulanda awoke with pain in her legs. She opened the door and rolled out onto the pavement of the parking lot.

"A cramp," she said, ". . . a bad cramp in my leg."

Djuan got up quickly to tend to Yulanda. He grabbed her leg and straightened it out, rubbing it as he pulled. "That's better," she said. "That hurt a lot."

"I will take care of you," he said as he gently helped her back into the car.

Yulanda noticed something strange about Djuan's care for her. He had seemed to react too strongly.

"It was only a cramp," she said. "Are you all right?"

"Don't talk about it," he replied.

Questions About the Story
MAIN IDEAS AND DETAILS
EXERCISE 8: Identifying Main Ideas

Circle the letter of the choice that best completes each sentence.

1. Rita is on the verge of two accomplishments:

    a. going to college and becoming a forest ranger

    b. passing the GED and becoming a forest ranger

    c. going out to dinner alone and finishing college

    d. passing the GED and becoming a police officer

2. Being a single parent and a student is a big change for Rita, and she feels

    a. entirely happy about getting divorced

    b. that she is doing an excellent job raising Sam

   c. pulled in at least three different directions

   d. that she'll never get involved with another man

3. Rita's leaving the restaurant before she has eaten shows that

   a. she has forgotten to bring a book or magazine

   b. people are making fun of her

   c. change can make simple things hard

   d. she couldn't afford anything on the menu

4. Djuan does not find work because

   a. he is old and cannot read or write English

   b. jobs are scarce and Djuan doesn't interview well

   c. he has a bad work record and a large family

   d. Tessa, Marissa, and Yulanda are all working

5. Djuan does not get involved in the illegal credit card scheme because

   a. it is dishonest

   b. his friend doesn't make much money

   c. he is afraid of getting caught

   d. he thinks it is a high-risk operation

EXERCISE 9: Fill in the Blank

Based on the reading, fill in the blanks with a word or phrase.

1. Rita tells Shirley she is seeing a _____.

2. Rita passes _____ out of _____ of the practice tests.

3. Tests indicate that Rita would like two things in a job: _____ and _____.

4. Rita is thinking about becoming a _____.

5. Rita had been married for _____ years.

6. Rita is trying to do three things at once: _____, _____, and _____.

7. Sam always wants to ride his _____ in the parking lot.

8. Rita has to stay with Sam while he is riding in the parking lot because Sam is so _____.

9. Rita has the feeling that something in her life is missing: _____ _____.

10. In Djuan's city, many industries are _____, there is high _____, and there are many _____ for every available job.

11. In the spring, Djuan's six months of _____ would be over.

12. Djuan and his family will try to make a living by _____ _____.

13. Djuan and his family plan on coming home _____.

14. Djuan thinks something is wrong with his car because he sees _____.

15. Yulanda has pain from _____ in the middle of the night.

READING BETWEEN THE LINES

EXERCISE 10: Understanding the Characters

> Authors often describe the behavior of characters without directly telling the reader what emotions or feelings the characters are experiencing.

Below are several excerpts and paraphrases from the reading. You are to "read between the lines" to identify what emotions the characters are feeling. In some cases, you may think the characters feel two or more emotions. It's fine to list more than one. Examples of emotions are listed on page 93, but if you think of other emotions, you can use them too.

After you have identified the emotion you think the character is experiencing, briefly explain why the character feels that way.

Emotions

shock	humor	grief
surprise	frustration	hate
anger	embarrassment	love
joy	sympathy	guilt
sorrow	loneliness	alarm
	fear	loyalty

1. Rita says her counselor's name is Liz. Shirley drops her coffee cup.

   a. What is Shirley feeling? *surprise*

   b. explanation: *Shirley didn't know that Liz had started working at the agency or that Rita was going there for counseling.*

2. At the restaurant, Rita feels that everyone notices that she is alone.

   a. What is Rita feeling?

   b. explanation:

3. Rita cannot shake the thought that her life should somehow be tied to a man.

   a. What is Rita feeling?

   b. explanation:

4. Sam speeds around the shopping center, laughing and talking to Rita.

   a. What is Sam feeling?

   b. explanation:

5. Djuan cannot seem to communicate his abilities in a job interview.

   a. What is he feeling?

   b. explanation:

6. "We can't work as fruit and vegetable pickers," says Marissa. "We lost Mama because we were picking."

   a. What is Marissa feeling?

   b. explanation:

7. Yulanda cries as they leave the city.

   a. What is she feeling?

   b. explanation:

8. Djuan notices that the car is having engine trouble.

   a. What is he feeling?

   b. explanation:

ANSWERS ARE ON PAGES 180-81.

CHAPTER 5
New Commitments

SCENE 1
Bob and Carol

That summer Bob and Carol were married in a flower garden on the grounds of her parents' church. The wedding was in August, during Carol's four-week vacation from her nursing school program.

In the months and weeks before her wedding day, Carol had tried to talk to her parents about how they might be involved in the planning and in the wedding itself. "We'll see," they kept saying. They would not even commit themselves to coming to the wedding. Finally, in exasperation, Carol asked her father point-blank if he would walk her down the aisle.

"We'll see," he mumbled again.

"If you don't say yes, I'll have to ask Uncle Joe," Carol replied. She realized that she had not disguised her irritation.

"I don't know," her father said.

"Then I'm asking Joe."

"You do what you want. You started doing whatever you wanted a long time ago anyway."

As they dressed for the wedding, Bob and his father both laughed about the idea of wearing tuxedoes because neither of them even owned a suit. They had some trouble figuring out how to assemble all the parts of the tuxedoes. In the end, Bob was impressed with his father's appearance. The old man had gotten a haircut and a shave the morning of the wedding and looked almost sophisticated in the tuxedo. He might even have passed for a rich man except for his hands, which were large and muscular—definitely a working man's hands.

Carol was far more nervous about the wedding than Bob. Most of her anxiety centered on whether or not her parents would attend. She had stayed at her Uncle Joe and Aunt Hilda's house the night before. They had stayed up late discussing the problem she had with her parents. Finally Joe called Carol's father. He tried to convince him to attend the wedding and walk Carol down the aisle. "I don't think so," her father had said.

The next afternoon, Carol arrived at the church a half hour before the wedding. She, her Aunt Hilda, and the bridesmaids went directly into the women's powder room at the back of the church. As they made last-minute adjustments to their gowns and hair, Carol heard loud noises coming from across the hall where the men were getting ready.

"God, don't let anything go wrong now," she thought. She knew Uncle Joe and her father were fighting. Very quickly the organ began to play, and the voices could no longer be heard.

At Carol's insistence, Hilda went across the hall to see if the men were all right. "Yeah, it's OK, I guess," someone said through the door.

Carol sat in the small powder room trying to fight back tears. Finally it was time for her to go to the garden. As she followed the bridesmaids into the garden, she saw that her father was there, standing with his brother Joe and dressed in a tuxedo. "They must have made up," she thought with some relief. Then she realized how embarrassing it would be for both her and her father if he were to be at the wedding but not walk her down the aisle.

As Carol approached the two men, she extended her left arm to Joe. But it was her father, not Joe, who took her arm to escort her. Carol held back for just an instant and looked at her father. She was searching for some sign from him that he accepted her, in spite of their differences. But her father would not look at her; rather, he gritted his teeth, kept his eyes on the front of the church, and gave a tug on her arm.

When she was alone with Bob for a moment after the ceremony she cried. "He's a rigid and stubborn fool," she sobbed. "I'll never know if he was here for me or because he thought it would be too embarrassing not to attend."

The reception took place that evening. Bob's father had rented the Veterans of Foreign Wars' Clubhouse and hired a band. Many people attended the dance, and they stayed long after Bob and Carol slipped away. Bob and Carol led off the dancing, followed by Carol's parents and Bob's father and his date.

At first Bob was impressed with his father's vitality and energy at the dance. But by ten-thirty Bob could see that the old man was running out of gas. He began to sit out some of the dances, and his ruddy face was ashen in color. "I hate to see him get this old," Bob thought. "I wonder how long he's going to be around!"

Bob and Carol had an exciting and carefree honeymoon. They went to New England, spending most of the time on the coast. When it rained, they stayed in hotels. When the weather was good, they camped in order to save money. They soon learned to tolerate and even enjoy each other's interests. Bob reluctantly agreed to go hear the Eastern Brass Quintet, a group that played classical music. The concert took place at a band shelter in a federal park next to the ocean. The fog rolled in off the water and it was so thick that they often couldn't even see the band, but both enjoyed the music immensely. By the same token, Carol was reluctant to go to the stock car races and "play the ponies," but she found that she liked both of these events.

They returned to find that Bob's boss had bought a second gas station. He asked if Bob were willing to be the manager of the second station. "I'll turn it over to you," he said. "You do the scheduling, the ordering, and the hiring and firing. I want to leave it pretty much in your hands. All I want is for the station to make a profit by the end of the year." Bob was happy to accept the responsibility, but he knew full well that running the station would be more than a full-time job. He'd be working more evenings and weekends than he had before.

During her second year in nurse's training, Carol's schedule changed. She spent less time in the classroom and began to work at the hospital. This often meant that Carol had classes in the morning and worked on a floor of the hospital at nights and on weekends.

A year went by, with Bob and Carol working hard and feeling successful both in their work and in their marriage. Carol's fear about being responsible for the lives of others was not totally gone. However, in her training she found that she was almost always part of a team of doctors, nurses, and nurses' aides. Consequently, it was not often that she alone was responsible for her patients.

One day, Carol unexpectedly bumped into Bob's father at the hospital. He'd been leaving the radiation therapy center and was clearly embarrassed and at a loss for words when they met. He looked at the ground for a moment, saying nothing. He got out his handkerchief and looked at Carol with moisture in his eyes. "I got cancer," he finally said. "I'm afraid it's gettin' the best of me."

Carol was shocked by the meeting. She returned later to read her father-in-law's medical record. He was right; it did look like he was dying of cancer. Later that afternoon Carol called the old man from work. "We've got to talk," she said. "This is not something that you should have to deal with by yourself. It's something I think you should talk to Bob about. It's important that he know."

"Would you tell him for me?" he asked. "I don't know how I could tell him."

"I can be there to help you and Bob," Carol replied, "but I think it's the kind of thing you'll have to discuss together." A lump had formed in Carol's throat. "Why don't you come over for dinner some evening this week and we'll talk about it."

When the old man came to dinner, the conversation was light and happy as he and Bob talked about old times. It was clear to Carol that Bob's father was avoiding the topic of his cancer. Finally, Carol said, "Bob, your father and I have something we have to talk to you about." Bob stopped talking and sat silently looking at the two. The old man looked to Carol for direction but said nothing. "You've got something to tell Bob," she said. The father clamped his jaw and looked at Carol helplessly.

"What is it?" asked Bob.

The old man turned and looked at Bob. As his old face softened, his eyes filled with tears, but still he said nothing.

"Your dad is being treated for cancer," Carol said to Bob.

Bob sat stunned. He knew from the old man's face that it was serious, and he immediately suspected that his father was dying.

Three weeks later, Carol once again needed to talk to Bob about something important. Two weeks earlier she had missed her period. At the time, she thought that the emotional stress surrounding Bob's father's illness had interrupted her cycle. But she had a test at the hospital and found that she was indeed pregnant. Having a baby was not a part of their plans at this time, and she had no idea how Bob would react. It wasn't that they didn't want to have children but rather that the timing was bad. They'd looked forward to the day when they'd both have full-time jobs. Bob was dreaming about buying a house and getting enough money together to open his own gas station. Besides, Carol had never really talked to Bob about getting pregnant. It probably had happened when she had not used her diaphragm. Consequently it could be seen as her fault.

Carol considered getting an abortion. If she did, she wouldn't have to face Bob with the problem of her mistake. But getting an abortion without even talking to Bob seemed unfair to him. After all, it was his child, too. Carol talked to a friend about her dilemma, and in that conversation she decided that she must share the problem with Bob.

One night after supper she got up the courage. "Bob," she said, "I've got something to tell you."

"What is it?"

"I should be happy, but I'm really more afraid . . . afraid I'm going to screw up our life. . . . Bob, I'm pregnant."

"Oh, God," said Bob. "How did that happen? We're so young and we're just getting started. . . ."

"I know. I didn't mean for it to happen."

"Are you sure?"

"Yes. I had the test."

"Damn! I just don't know what to say. How could this happen?"

"I just didn't always use the diaphragm."

"How dumb can you get? You're a nurse. You know what you have to do!"

"It wasn't smart."

"What the hell do we do now?"

"I've thought about it a lot the last couple of days. Either I get an abortion or we become parents. I honestly don't know how I feel about abortions."

"God, what a decision to make. There's so much I want to have and do. But we're talking about a life. . . . I can't help but think about my old man, who's hanging on to life with everything he's got."

"If you want to get technical about it, the medical profession doesn't really look at it as being life until it has a heartbeat."

"Well, I don't really want to be too technical," said Bob. "Somehow it just wouldn't feel right for you to have an abortion when my old man is checking out. It feels better to think about someone else checking in. I think we can still have our dreams. The world is full of working mothers."

"OK," said Carol. "I think I can rise to the occasion."

Death came slowly to Bob's father. He never talked about it, but his life changed. At times, he'd spend long periods of time reminiscing and "mending fences" with the rest of the family and friends. He made out a will. He also had flurries of activity when he'd work beyond his strength but claim he never felt better. On these occasions, he literally collapsed at night.

The hospital experience was most difficult. The illness finally progressed to the point where he needed to be hospitalized. The cancer had started to interfere with his kidneys. Now the energy that he'd begun to show turned to bitterness and anger. The confinement was unavoidable, but the old man raged against it. He treated the hospital staff as if he had been unjustly sent to prison and they were the guards.

Bob and Carol fared no better. Whatever they did seemed to go wrong. He complained that they got there too early or too late. When Bob slipped him a half pint of whiskey, he said he'd rather have vodka. Bob found himself terribly angry at his father at a time when he desperately wanted their relationship to be at its best.

As time went on, though, his father's mood changed. He began asking to see Carol and delighted in her pregnancy.

"Is it a boy or a girl?" he'd asked.

"I don't know. The doctor says a boy."

"How the hell does he know?"

"He says boys' hearts beat slower."

"I say it's a girl with a big heart. How do you like that?"

"Fine."

"I'd be willing to put money on it. If I live to see a granddaughter, I promise I'll give her a $1,000 savings bond. She can cash it sometime and think of the old man who always wanted a daughter. I would have loved the hell out of her."

"I hope that all happens," said Carol. "We'll plan on it being a girl for you."

Finally, there came a point when the old man's health slipped fast. He was quiet and depressed. Three weeks before the baby was due, his kidneys shut down. The doctor told Bob and Carol that he would die within five days. Five days later he was full of energy. He rallied.

"I haven't taken a leak in five days," he said. "I'm one of the only humans living who doesn't have to waste time with that kind of stuff." He lived another six days appearing healthy and at peace. He seemed reconciled to the fact of his coming death.

The old man died seventeen days before his granddaughter was born.

SCENE 2
Paul

Paul heard people in the front hall yelling that the police had arrived. "Happy eighteenth birthday from the local pig pen," he said. "Now, how the hell do I get out of here?" They opened a window and pushed out the screen. Paul squatted on the sill looking down at the ground sixteen feet below. "It's a long way down there," he said. "I'll break my back." Somebody got a blanket and held one end while Paul let himself down the length of the blanket. Then he dropped the rest of the way and hit the ground running. His right arm shot up as if he were waving good-bye, but he never even turned around. It would be months before anyone heard from Paul again.

He hid for two days, spending most of his time in the attic of a friend's garage. He went to the grocery store for food at night. Not even his friend knew he was there. Finally, afraid to contact Annie or any of his friends, he arranged a ride with an acquaintance to the next town. From there he took a bus to Chicago, which for months was to be his new home.

But Chicago was a tough town to survive in without connections. Friends were hard to come by. If he operated by himself, Paul might cross into someone else's territory. "I'm more afraid of my own kind than the police," he thought.

Finally he solved the problem by buying a car and operating in the suburbs around Chicago. He spent the early part of the evening cruising through neighborhoods looking for houses to rob. He went in as soon as it was dark and then never returned to the same neighborhood. He always fenced the goods in downtown Chicago, far from the suburbs where the goods were taken.

Paul talked to Annie several times, calling from pay phones outside of Chicago. "Things can't ever be the same," she said. "You're on the run and I'm here. . . . You can't come back for years." They figured that she couldn't join Paul unless she changed her identity, and she wasn't willing to take such an extreme measure. Finally she told Paul that they were through and that she had to get on with her life. "I guess I've known for a long time that it would come to this," she said. "When you wouldn't get a job, I figured that it was just a matter of time. . . ."

But Paul was persistent, so much so that one night he made the trip back to see Annie. She opened the door hesitantly after he said who he was. As Paul entered his old apartment, Annie took his arm and ushered him in. "Paul, do you remember Jamie? Jamie, this is Paul." Paul was startled. It hadn't occurred to him that Annie would have another man move in. But he looked around and realized that the men's clothing hanging in the room was Jamie's, not his own.

He'd met Jamie before at the restaurant where Annie worked. After he and Jamie exchanged polite greetings, he turned back to Annie. "Can we go somewhere?" he asked.

"It's really too late." she said.

"It's only nine o'clock."

"That's not what I meant. There's nothing left to do, Paul. Talk would just make things worse. I'm with Jamie now, and that's the way it has to be."

Paul put his arm around Annie's shoulder as if he were trying to lead her out the door. She stiffened slightly and looked at Jamie. Paul stopped, dropped his arm, and turned to face Annie.

"Good-bye," he said.

"Good-bye," she said. "Good luck, Paul. . . . You're going to need it."

Paul stopped as soon as Annie shut the door behind him. Reaching into his jacket, he pulled out a joint. Lighting it, he breathed deeply and held in the smoke for as long as he could. He'd feel better in a minute, he thought.

Questions About the Story
MAIN IDEAS AND DETAILS
EXERCISE 1: Main Ideas and Supporting Evidence

Circle the letter of the choice that best completes each sentence. Provide at least one piece of evidence from the story that supports your answer. The first one is done for you as an example.

1. Before Carol's wedding, her parents
   a. say they won't attend the wedding
   b. ask her Uncle Joe to walk Carol down the aisle
   (c.) won't promise to attend the wedding
   d. ask the minister not to marry Bob and Carol

   Evidence: *They would not commit themselves to come. Uncle Joe called Carol's father to try to convince him to attend.*

2. Just before the wedding, Carol is about to cry because
   a. she is so happy
   b. Aunt Hilda has left her alone
   c. neither of her parents are there
   d. her father and uncle are fighting

   Evidence:

3. At the dance after the wedding, Bob's father
   a. is too embarrassed to dance
   b. is alone and not having a good time
   c. is energetic at first but tired later
   d. has too much to drink and goes to sleep

   Evidence:

4. When Bob and Carol return from their honeymoon, Bob's boss
   a. asks Bob to manage a gas station
   b. tells Bob he is quitting the business
   c. gives Bob and Carol a late wedding present
   d. asks Bob where he's been for the last two weeks

   Evidence:

5. Carol finds out that Bob's father is dying of cancer

   a. when Bob and his father tell her

   b. because he looks so weak

   c. because his doctor calls her about it

   d. when she runs into him at the hospital

   Evidence:

6. Before Paul leaves for Chicago, he

   a. calls Annie to let her know where he will be

   b. comes back to get some of his things

   c. buys a car

   d. hides out and doesn't contact his friends

   Evidence:

7. Annie does not join Paul because

   a. she doesn't know where he is

   b. she would have to change her identity

   c. she decides she doesn't like him

   d. she is afraid the police are watching her

   Evidence:

8. When Paul returns to see Annie, she doesn't want to spend time with him because

   a. she is afraid the police will see them together

   b. she considers their relationship to be over

   c. she is afraid of Jamie

   d. she has to get ready to go to work

   Evidence:

EXERCISE 2: Fill in the Blank

Complete the following sentences by providing details from the story.

1. Bob and Carol's wedding is in the month of _____.

2. Bob's father's hands are _____ and

_____.

3. Carol stays at _____ and _____'s house the night before the wedding.

4. As Carol enters the garden, she extends her arm to _____ _____.

5. _____ walks Carol down the aisle.

6. Bob suspects that his father is dying because of _____ _____.

7. When Carol discovers she is pregnant, she and Bob decide to _____ _____.

8. After his birthday party, Paul hides for two days in _____ _____.

9. Paul goes to _____.

10. The houses Paul robs are in _____.

EXERCISE 3: **True or False**

Below are statements about the story. Indicate whether they are true or false by writing a *T* or *F* in the blank.

_____ **1.** The wedding reception is at the Knights of Columbus Hall.

_____ **2.** Carol and Bob go to Chicago for their honeymoon.

_____ **3.** Carol discovers that she likes the stock car races.

_____ **4.** Bob is entirely happy about Carol's pregnancy.

_____ **5.** Bob's father dies soon after his kidneys fail.

_____ **6.** Paul jumps the entire sixteen feet to the ground.

_____ **7.** Paul sells his stolen goods in downtown Chicago.

_____ **8.** In Chicago, Paul is most afraid of the police.

APPLICATION

EXERCISE 4: **Stages of Accepting Death**

People seem to go through five distinct stages in coming to accept their own deaths. Bob's father goes through these stages, which are listed on page 104. List his feelings and actions that correspond to the five stages. Use a separate sheet of paper.

1. shock and denial
2. rage and anger
3. making bargains

4. depression
5. peace and acceptance

EXERCISE 5: Your Experiences with Death

Place a check mark in front of the answer that most closely reflects your attitude or experience. If none of the answers provided are true for you, write your own answer in the blank space provided. If possible, discuss your answers with others in your class.

1. When I was young, the subject of death was talked about in my family

———   **a.** openly

———   **b.** with some discomfort

———   **c.** only when necessary

———   **d.** as though it were a forbidden subject

———   **e.** _____

———   **f.** I can't recall any discussion.

2. My idea of what happens after death is best described as

———   **a.** heaven and hell

———   **b.** reincarnation

———   **c.** a sleep

———   **d.** end of all physical and mental activity

———   **e.** mysterious and unknowable

———   **f.** _____

———   **g.** I have no idea.

3. My present attitudes toward dying have been most influenced by

———   **a.** the death of someone close to me

———   **b.** things I have read

———   **c.** my religious upbringing

———   **d.** introspection and meditation

———   **e.** rituals such as funerals or wakes

———   **f.** television and movies

———   **g.** my state of health

———   **h.** _____

4. To me, the worst aspect of death would be that I would

_____ **a.** no longer be able to experience life

_____ **b.** have no control over what happened to my body

_____ **c.** not know what I would be facing after death

_____ **d.** no longer be able to care for my family

_____ **e.** cause grief to my family and friends

_____ **f.** _____

5. I feel that a fatally ill or brain-dead person should be

_____ **a.** kept alive as long as possible

_____ **b.** treated according to his or her own wishes or those of the immediate family

_____ **c.** permitted to die a natural death

_____ **d.** _____

6. If my physician knew that I were terminally ill, I

_____ **a.** would not want to know

_____ **b.** would want to know

7. If I had a terminal illness, I would

_____ **a.** not want anyone to know

_____ **b.** tell people who are close to me but not discuss it

_____ **c.** discuss it openly with people who are close to me

_____ **d.** be willing to discuss it openly with anyone

_____ **e.** _____

8. If someone close to me were dying and wanted to talk to me about it, I would feel

_____ **a.** too embarrassed to talk

_____ **b.** uncomfortable but willing

_____ **c.** at ease

_____ **d.** too upset to talk

_____ **e.** _____

9. When I think about how my own life will end, I most fear

——   **a.**   having to endure a long debilitating illness

——   **b.**   being killed in an accident

——   **c.**   facing what lies after death

——   **d.**   being killed in a violent incident

——   **e.**   the difficulties of old age

——   **f.**   dying in a nuclear war

——   **g.**   _____

10. If you were told that you had only a limited time to live, how would you want to spend the time you had left?

——   **a.**   I would become more withdrawn: reading, contemplating, or praying.

——   **b.**   I would spend my time helping others.

——   **c.**   I would complete projects and tie up loose ends.

——   **d.**   I would continue my life in my usual way.

——   **e.**   I would try to accomplish one very important thing.

——   **f.**   I would commit suicide.

——   **g.**   I would travel around and say good-bye to all my family and friends.

——   **h.**   _____

ANSWERS ARE ON PAGE 181.

SCENE 3
Ted and Liz

Ted recovered from the accident quickly. Within several days of the accident, the pain was gone, though he still felt tired most of the time. His doctor encouraged him to be up and around as much as he could. The doctor even suggested that he take half-hour walks around the hospital and outside. The major problem for Ted was his appearance. He was reluctant to be seen because about half his head was shaved and the rest of his hair was cut very short. He found a floppy-brimmed hat with a beer company's name on it, and he wore the hat constantly except when he was sleeping.

When friends dropped in to see him, they almost always stopped at the nurse's station to ask what room he was in. Ted quickly learned to hear the nurses directing someone to his room. Hearing his room number mentioned served as an early warning signal. Ted would make sure he was dressed for a visitor, including his hat.

Each time he heard that someone was coming, he began to panic. He thought the person might be Elizabeth McKenna. But the days slipped away, and the doctor told him that he would soon be going home. Still Elizabeth did not visit him. Then, on the evening before he was getting out of the hospital, she suddenly appeared in his doorway. Ted reached quickly for his hat.

"Oh hi," he said. "I didn't hear you coming."

"I didn't have to ask where you were because I was here before. Do you remember me? I was here with my Dad late last week. . . . I'm Liz McKenna. . . . You were still kind of out of it."

"Oh yeah," said Ted, ". . . I think I remember you."

"I saw your accident—I was jogging."

"My mother said she thought you stopped the bleeding."

"You looked like you were hurt pretty bad. I didn't know what to do except to apply pressure."

Ted pictured himself lying in the front seat of his car with Liz holding his head. "I sure want to thank you," he said. "I don't know what would have happened if you hadn't come along."

"Well, there's something I want to tell you. You don't really have to thank me," she said. "I think I did it more for myself than for you. . . . It's hard to explain."

"I don't understand."

"You're a student, right?"

"Yeah."

"Well, I don't know about you, but I've been thinking lately that I don't like being a student. It's not that I don't like the schoolwork. For me, the problem is that I'm always preparing to do something that's going to happen in the future. I'm never doing anything that's very important today . . . in the present. Anyway, as I look back on my first year at the University, the most important things I did were working as a counselor and helping you. I can see the effect because you're here and you're OK."

"Oh geez, what do I say?"

"Nothing. I mean it. I think I did it more for me than for you."

They talked about Ted's job, about the McKenna family business, and about their high school classmates. In spite of Ted's anxiety about what he might say to Liz, he found her very easy to talk to. Seldom had he found anybody as open and unguarded in conversation as Liz.

When she was about to leave, she asked if he liked to sail. "I don't know. I've never done it," he replied.

"I'll call you sometime," she said. "I go with my parents sometimes, and the boat's big enough to take more people."

After she left, Ted tried to remember the details of Liz's visit. Up to now he'd been captivated only by her appearance because he knew nothing else about her. Now he realized that he'd been so wrapped up in talking to her that he'd almost forgotten how pretty she was. "Well, not quite," he thought, remembering her long legs and finely cut face.

Ted returned to work, wearing his hat. It was two weeks after his accident. At the end of the day, Mr. McKenna stopped in to see how he was doing. The boss mentioned that the incident had been good for his daughter. "She said that it made her realize how much she wants to do something worthwhile with her life. She also talked about taking you along sometime when we go sailing. How about the first weekend of next month? We're going for the full weekend, and we'll sleep on the boat."

Ted told Mr. McKenna that he'd like to go, but later he began to have second thoughts. Mr. McKenna was probably a millionaire. The McKenna family was certainly in a different league than he was. He remembered something from a book he'd read in a high school English class: the rich are different. There was another matter, too, that troubled Ted. What was Liz thinking of when she had asked him to go sailing? Was she attracted to him? Or did she think of him as just a friend? Or was she still feeling sorry for him because of the accident?

Although he was very nervous, he called Liz and asked her if they could talk about the trip over pizza. When they got together, Liz was in a jovial mood. They joked and laughed, mainly about the problems they had trying to be successful University students. Several times during the conversation, Liz reached out and touched Ted's arm or hand. His expectations soared as he convinced himself that Liz had a romantic interest in him. His fantasies ran wild during the week before the trip.

The McKennas picked up Ted at his apartment early Saturday morning. Mrs. McKenna had the same slim and finely chiseled appearance as Liz and could have passed for her older sister. She also talked to Ted in the same forthright way that Liz had. The questions she asked might have seemed too personal for a first meeting. But coming from her, they didn't bother Ted. She seemed genuinely interested in him and his point of view. She didn't seem to judge or evaluate what he said.

Once on board the boat, they stored the food and then their belongings. Ted would sleep in the forward compartment. The three McKennas would have the main cabin, which was the galley and living room during the day but converted into a sleeping area at night. Though the trip hadn't even begun, one of Ted's fantasies was already dashed upon the rocks. He had imagined himself at least sleeping in the same cabin as Liz.

The plan for the day was to sail east and arrive by nightfall on a cluster of small, uninhabited islands. The islands would provide shelter for the boat during the night. White clouds drifted overhead, signaling the direction of the wind. Small whitecaps rose on the surface of the water, indicating it would be a fast sail.

The McKennas worked well together rigging the sails. Ted stood by somewhat helplessly, not knowing what to do and not wanting to be in the way. Once they were under way, Liz went into the cabin to change clothes. Ted sat with Mr. McKenna as he steered the boat. "Tell me what it's like to work for the McKenna Company," he said to Ted.

"Geez. What do I say?" Ted replied. "I like it a lot. Not many people my age have the chance to do something where you can learn so much."

"You must be doing a good job because you've come a long way from working in the blueprint room. How ambitious are you, anyway? What do you want to be doing in ten years?"

The question caught Ted off guard. He hesitated for a minute. "I don't really know," he said.

"I guess I didn't know either when I was your age. Do you know how I started my business? I built a house for the family. I bought a hammer and borrowed a circular saw from a friend and worked every night and weekend. I had to go to everyone for advice. A guy at the lumberyard and some friends taught me most of what I had to know about building.

"When the house was done, I realized that it was worth about twice as much as I put into it, so I decided to build another one and sell it. This time I hired a carpenter to help. Together we got the job done in four months. Then I figured I was on the right track. I started three houses at the same time and hired carpenters and plumbers to do the work. I just managed the operation and did the planning and buying. Well, to make a long story short, I spent a lot of time thinking about how things could be done better or more efficiently. I finally decided that with the right design, I could build better buildings in a factory. Then the pieces could be shipped to the site to be assembled."

"So you really started from scratch," Ted said.

"Well, I did and I didn't," Mr. McKenna said. "I didn't have much money. But on the other hand, I had a real good credit rating. I never missed a payment on a bill, we kept out of debt, and I banked at the same bank for a long time. I guess I had a good reputation at the bank. As it turned out, that was almost as good as having a lot of money. In fact, I still think my reputation is more important than money."

"I heard a story about how you once built a building for an accounting firm and that when you were done, the firm didn't like it, so you built them a new one."

"Yeah. That's what we did."

"Just to make them happy."

"We had a contract, and we'd built it just the way they wanted. Legally they had to keep the building. But I wanted to be sure that they were satisfied, so we went back to the drawing board. I had to hang onto the first building for a while, but we didn't lose much in the process. But you know, that story has really gotten around. It's the best advertising I could have gotten because we're seen as trustworthy."

Liz and her mother joined Ted and her father at the back of the boat. "We were talking about Ted's work, and I just told him my life story," Mr. McKenna laughed.

"Rags to riches," Liz said with a smile.

"Not exactly," her father replied. "We were really talking about how I found out what I wanted to do for a living."

"Did it really just happen?" Liz asked. "Or do you think you planned it?"

"I didn't have any kind of master plan, if that's what you mean. It was like going down a path that had all these little forks in the road. I just kept making a lot of seemingly small decisions until suddenly I had a sense of where I was headed."

"But something must have given you a sense of direction," Ted said. "It all came together so perfectly."

"I think you just have to do as well as you possibly can at whatever you're doing at the moment," Mr. McKenna said. "But at the same time, you look for opportunities. Or you make them for yourself if you have to."

"That sounds good," Liz's mother replied, ". . . but what if things don't pop into place? How many jobs are there that are really challenging or meaningful?"

"Maybe all of them," Mr. McKenna replied.

"Aw, come off it! The world is full of people who get no satisfaction from their work," said Liz.

"I'll grant you that," said Mr. McKenna. "There are congressmen and university professors and plumbers and truck drivers who are miserable. But my point is that in every occupation there are a lot of people who take great pride in what they do. That means that it may not be the job. Maybe it's the way people think about their work that really counts. Ted has come a long way with our company because of the way he thought about the job. He made the opportunity for himself. We've had a half dozen other print boys that worked for a semester and then left. There has to be something inside the person that pushes them. Then the job takes on a different meaning."

"What about me?" Liz asked.

"You've got it, Liz. You just don't know what to do with it yet," said her mother, laughing.

It was necessary to change the direction they were sailing. Liz and Ted went forward to swing the jib. On the horizon, the islands they were sailing to could barely be seen.

"Pretty heavy conversation," Liz said to Ted. "Does it bother you?"

"Not at all," Ted said. "But I'm not used to it. My parents never seemed to talk about anything."

"Well, don't let them overwhelm you with their talk."

By the middle of the afternoon, they approached the islands and anchored in a sheltered cove. When the sails were taken down, the women went to the cabin to change into their swimming suits. Ted and Mr. McKenna changed on the deck. The water was cold, and the four hesitated before jumping in. "Grab the person next to you," said Mr. McKenna, "and we'll all go in together." Liz wrapped an arm around Ted's neck and the four teetered for a moment on the edge. Then they plunged into the lake.

They pulled a rubber raft into the water and began to play a version of "king of the mountain." Everyone scrambled to monopolize the raft. Ted had been very aware of Liz's having a sinewy kind of strength about her. In this game he found that she was even stronger than she appeared, and her mother and father were strong as well. Though he was bashful about playing the game, Ted was soon trying his hardest to control the raft. At one point he found himself kneeling on one end of the raft with Liz on the other end. They reached for each other and ended up hugging and struggling at the same time. The older McKennas toppled the raft, sending Ted and Liz into the water.

After swimming, they grilled steaks for supper on the rear of the boat. Then Mrs. McKenna played the guitar as the rest listened. The sun sank in the west and stars began to appear. Ted and Liz stayed up after her parents went to bed. They put on jackets because it was cool, and a fog bank rolled at them from the center of the lake.

"You're amazing," said Ted. "Not just you, but your parents, too."

"I don't know," she said, "I sometimes wonder what we'd be like if Daddy hadn't been successful."

"You might not have this boat, but you'd still be the same people."

"I've had the chance to do some things that I might not have had otherwise," she said. She talked for a long time about her wilderness experience. When she finished telling about the thoughts she'd had as she sat neck deep in the snow, she asked Ted if they made any sense to him.

"I think I know what you mean," he said. "It's hard to know what's important. Maybe your father's right. . . . Maybe you've got to see the importance in whatever you're doing at the moment." They sat next to each other for a long time, each looking up at the stars and each conscious of the other's presence, but each lost in private thoughts.

Questions About the Story
MAIN IDEAS AND DETAILS
EXERCISE 6: Recalling the Story in Your Own Words

Complete the following in a few phrases or sentences. Each question asks you to identify main ideas and supporting details about Mr. McKenna and his family.

1. Mr. McKenna started his business by
   (*give at least three details*)

2. Mr. McKenna places great value on

   a.

   b.

3. Mr. McKenna thinks people find value in their work by

   a.

   b.

4. The McKenna family has the following characteristics:

   a.

   b.

   c.

EXERCISE 7: Cause and Effect

Often you can get insight into characters by looking for what causes their feelings and actions. You can also understand events and circumstances better by looking for their causes.

Complete the following sentences by writing down the cause for the action or feeling you are given.

1. Ted panics each time someone approaches his hospital room because

2. Ted does not have his hat on when Liz appears at his door because

3. Liz feels that helping Ted has done more for her than for Ted because

4. Ted has second thoughts about going sailing with the McKennas because
    (give three causes)

5. Ted doesn't mind when Mrs. McKenna asks him personal questions because
    (give two causes)

6. Mr. McKenna got a good credit rating because
    (give three causes)

APPLICATION

EXERCISE 8: A Question of Value

Read the following passage and answer the questions that follow in a few sentences or phrases. If possible, discuss your answers with others in your class.

Mr. McKenna's Dilemma

Mr. McKenna's company designed a building for a group of doctors who were starting a new medical clinic. The doctors were already very wealthy, and one reason they were building the clinic was that they wanted a tax shelter. Because of their tax situation, the new clinic would end up costing the doctors very little.

A contract was drawn up and signed, and work began on the clinic. It was to cost $430,000. The doctors had already made a $100,000 down payment. Then one day one of Mr. McKenna's accountants discovered that he had made a $50,000 mistake and that the company should have charged $380,000 instead of $430,000 for the clinic.

At a company meeting, everybody urged Mr. McKenna to keep the extra $50,000.

"They'll never know the difference . . . and besides, they just write the whole thing off their taxes," people said.

"But we've overcharged them," Mr. McKenna replied. "Don't we have an obligation to charge all customers the same?"

1. Based on the reading, briefly describe Mr. McKenna's philosophy toward his customers.

2. Taking the extra $50,000 from the doctors would violate Mr. McKenna's philosophy. However, the contract has already been signed. What should he do? Why?

ANSWERS ARE ON PAGES 181-82.

SCENE 4
Rita

Several times a day, Rita found herself searching down the street for the mailman. It had been almost a month since she had applied and interviewed for the police force academy. She was in great suspense waiting for a reply.

Then, on a Saturday while Rita was visiting with Liz, the letter came. Upon discovering the letter, Rita's heart began to pound. "I can't open it," she thought. "I'm counting on it so much . . . I won't be able to take it if I'm rejected." She held her breath and stared at the envelope. Carrying it to the kitchen, she took out a knife and carefully cut open the top. Again holding her breath, she closed her eyes, drew out the letter, and held it in front of her until she had to gasp for air.

Rita opened her eyes and scanned the letter quickly, still afraid of what it might say. She turned to the second page. Then she breathed a sigh of relief, and a broad smile swept across her face. On the second page was a clear and unmistakable acceptance—the title on the page said "Exercises to Do in Preparation for the Police Academy."

Rita laughed and threw the letter into the air. Retrieving it, she ran outside to share the good news with Sam. "We did it," she yelled. "Sammy, come here!" The neighbor from next door gave Rita a funny look. "Isn't Sam with his dad?" she asked.

"Oh, you're right," said Rita sheepishly. "I'm not thinking. . . . I'm too excited. . . . I just got me a J-O-B as a C-O-P. I'm going to be a real working woman with a real good job."

"Just what this city needs . . . another wacked-out cop," the neighbor said under her breath.

Rita rushed back to the telephone and dialed the number of the agency. She hoped that Liz was still there. "I'm absolutely delighted," Liz said. "I wish all our clients were as successful as you . . . but, Rita, you know that the training program isn't going to be easy."

It wasn't easy. The training program was a physical and academic challenge. The classroom training involved courses in law, psychology, arrest procedures, and even English. And in the other half of the program, the trainee met all kinds of physical challenges. These included conditioning exercises, classes in how to subdue a criminal, practice in the use of a variety of weapons, and driving during pursuit of a criminal. In all phases of the training, the women attending the academy were treated identically to, and were expected to perform as well as, the men.

Rita's training was difficult for Sam. Rita had arranged for him to go to a day-care center when she began the academy. He cried when she took him there each day, and it was clear that he did not like that part of the plan. And to make matters worse, he began to cause trouble for the day-care center staff. Each day when she returned from the academy, Rita would get a fresh report on Sam's activities: "He was using that bad 'F' word," or "Sam took off his clothes today, and we had to chase him while he ran around the yard naked."

Rita was concerned. Was Sam going to react badly to the day-care center? Was it going to cause permanent problems for him to grow up with an absent father and a working mother? Or was his behavior only temporary and a normal reaction to having his mother, who had always been present, suddenly go off to work?

Later, however, there came a point when Sam's behavior changed for the better.

After twelve weeks at the police academy, those trainees who were still in the program began working in the community. Entering this phase of training was no small occasion. For the first time, the cadets were issued standard police uniforms. From that day on, Rita dropped off and picked up Sam in uniform.

On her first day in uniform, Sam had taken her by the hand and begged her to come into the day-care center with him. As they entered, it became clear to Rita why Sam had wanted her to come in. He had begun to take great pride in her and in the fact that she was becoming a police officer.

After that, Sam's behavior improved. "I guess he's decided that he and his mama are going to be OK," Rita told Shirley.

"Oh God, yes," Shirley replied. "He's so proud of you the buttons should be poppin' off his shirt. Now he don't want to do anything to make you feel bad. . . . I know, 'cause Sam and I talk about it, and I feel just like he does."

SCENE 5
Djuan

As Djuan and his family drove, the grayness of the Northern spring gave way to the greenness of the South. Now they had to stop about every hundred miles to add oil to the car. Soon they were passing fields in which vegetables were being harvested. Djuan was excited. It had been almost six months since he'd had the challenge of hard work. He wondered if he could pick as well as he had when he'd first come to America.

The long trip was difficult for Yulanda because of her pregnancy. She felt exhausted but would not eat, and Djuan worried about her. He wanted to get settled somewhere as soon as possible.

The names of the northern Florida towns were familiar to Djuan. He knew the location of an employment center where they could find out about available work in the fields. There, through a telephone call, the center arranged work for the family. Then they set off in the direction of the farm that would be their first job site.

The manager of the farm and Djuan talked for a short time while the family waited in the car. Then he led them to living quarters that the farm provided for seasonal help. As Djuan and his family followed in the car, the manager walked ahead up a dirt path just wide enough for the car. "You got a problem with that car," the manager said. "Too much smoke. Engine's worn out."

Three identical buildings came into view. They were concrete block houses, each built to hold two families or groups of pickers. The bathrooms were in another smaller building behind the house.

"You've got running water, 'lectricity, and a hot plate," the manager explained. "We've got ice over by my house if you have to keep things cold."

In their side of the building was one large room with a concrete floor. Two sleeping areas were created by four-foot-high walls that partly divided the room. The furniture consisted of six cots and a table for eating, which was surrounded by four chairs. "Yulanda and I will sleep here," said Djuan as he pushed two of the cots together. "You kids will sleep there," he said, pointing to the back of the room. "We'll use the extra bed for a sofa."

The family took out bedrolls and put them on the soiled mattresses that lay on each cot. It had been a very long drive, and they were content to stretch out on their bedrolls. Almost immediately the children were asleep. Djuan and Yulanda lay next to each other in silence.

Finally Yulanda spoke. "You happy with this place?" she asked.

"It looks like we may get three weeks of work," he replied. "Tomatoes. They ripen slowly."

Yulanda moved her bedroll over so that it was touching Djuan's and then put an arm around his neck.

"Djuan," she said, "You are a working man. I know how hard it was with no job. . . . You are happier now. . . . I can tell." She moved even closer and began to unbutton his shirt.

Djuan turned and looked at his young wife. A frown crept across his face.

"We have to get some money," he said. "I hate picking vegetables . . . but here we are, and we'll go home in the fall with money."

"Now you sound sad. I don't want you sad," she said. She threw one leg over Djuan and then sat up, on top of him. Then she punched lightly at his ribs, tickling him. Djuan smiled and started to laugh. She immediately covered his mouth with her hand. "No noise," she said, indicating that she didn't want to wake the children. Djuan moved her hand away from his mouth and then pulled her face next to his. "We take good care of each other," he said.

"What you mean?" she asked.

"Nothing bad happens," he answered. "We get our money, and we all get home safe." Yulanda put both arms under Djuan's head and began lightly kissing his face.

They were awakened by the sound of a tractor pulling wagons toward the fields. After a hasty breakfast, just as it was getting light, Djuan, Yulanda, and Tessa followed the wagon tracks to the field. Marissa stayed behind to care for Carlo.

They would work as a team, with two people picking and one carrying the baskets back and forth between the pickers and the wagon. At the wagon, the tomatoes were weighed and the basket emptied.

Partway through the morning, it became clear that Tessa was a much slower worker than Djuan. To make the most money, he would have to pick, and Tessa and

Yulanda would have to take turns hauling the baskets back to the wagon. After lunch, while Carlo took his nap, Marissa also worked. By dusk, Djuan figured that together they had made $83. Renting the living quarters cost $6 per day. Food would cost about $10 per day. All the money that was left went into the cigar box, locked in the trunk of the car.

That evening they still had to shop for groceries. Long after dark they ate their evening meal. "I didn't remember how hard picking is," Tessa said. "I may fall asleep while I'm eating."

"You did good," Djuan said. "We all did good. . . . You think we can work six days a week?" Yulanda nodded, saying that they would, but her legs and her back had begun to get stiff. She was so tired that she was having trouble eating.

On the third day of picking, right in the middle of the afternoon, the manager told all the workers that there would be no more picking that day. The tractor used to pull the loaded wagons out of the field had broken down. If the tomatoes were picked and left on the wagon in the field, they'd rot in the heat. Picking would begin again after the tractor had been fixed.

Later that afternoon while Djuan's family was resting, the manager knocked on the door of their living quarters. When Djuan saw who it was, his first thought was that the manager was telling the workers to leave. But the manager had something else in mind. "I gotta get that tractor workin' soon," he said, "or we'll lose the harvest. Trouble is, it's a two-man job. You done any mechanics?"

"I've used tools," Djuan replied. "I worked at a foundry for three years."

"I was thinkin' that with some help, I might be able to have the tractor workin' by tomorrow."

"I can help. . . ."

"I'll tell you what. I noticed how bad your car was smokin'. I was thinking that if we could do the tractor now, later, if you want, we'll fix your car."

Djuan took directions from the manager as they spent the evening taking apart the tractor engine. The next morning they were waiting at the auto parts store when it opened to purchase new pistons, rings, and bearings. The manager sent the workers back into the fields as he and Djuan worked to assemble the engine. By noon, the tractor was back in use, hauling a wagon load out of the field.

"Not bad," the manager told Djuan. "That job would have cost me $800 at the dealer's. We did it for 'bout $200 almost overnight. You got a knack for mechanics. I wouldn't have guessed that you never worked on engines before."

Questions About the Story
MAIN IDEAS AND DETAILS

EXERCISE 9: Main Ideas and Supporting Evidence

Below are some of the main ideas from the chapter. Below each main idea, write in evidence from the reading that supports it.

1. Rita really wants to be accepted on the police force.

   Evidence:

   a.

   b.

   c.

2. Liz has become an important person in Rita's life.

   Evidence:

3. The police training program is difficult.

   Evidence:

   a.

   b.

   c.

4. Sam is proud of Rita's becoming a policewoman.

   Evidence:

   a.

   b.

5. The housing provided for Djuan and other seasonal help has only the barest essentials.

Evidence:

a.

b.

c.

6. Harvesting tomatoes is very hard work.

Evidence:

a.

b.

c.

7. Djuan has a talent for working on engines.

Evidence:

a.

b.

EXERCISE 10: Sequence

Number the following events in the order in which they occurred in the lives of the characters.

Rita

_____   **a.**   Sam began attending a day-care center.

_____   **b.**   Rita got a police uniform.

_____   **c.**   Rita applied and interviewed for the police academy.

_____   **d.**   Sam's behavior at the day-care center improved.

_____   **e.**   Rita received a letter of acceptance from the police academy.

_____   **f.**   Sam had problems at the day-care center.

Djuan

_____   **a.**   Djuan's family went to an employment center.

_____   **b.**   Yulanda tickled Djuan.

_____   **c.**   Djuan helped fix the tractor.

_____   **d.**   They began work in the fields.

_____   **e.**   The tractor broke down.

_____   **f.**   Djuan and his family drove south.

_____   **g.**   They shopped for groceries.

_____   **h.**   They went to a farm.

VOCABULARY

EXERCISE 11: Synonyms

> A **synonym** is a word (or sometimes a phrase) that means almost the same thing as another word.

In the phrases below, a word is underlined. In the blank provided, write a synonym for the word. Then use the *original underlined word* in a sentence of your own. The first one is done for you.

1. . . . it had been <u>almost</u> a month   *close to*
    He's been missing for <u>almost</u> a year.

2. She was in <u>suspense</u> waiting for a reply.   _____

3. I won't be able to take it if I'm <u>rejected</u>.   _____

4. . . . <u>retrieving</u> the letter   _____

5. "You're right," said Rita <u>sheepishly</u>.   _____

6. I'm <u>absolutely</u> delighted.   _____

7. Women were treated <u>identically</u> to men.   _____

8. Entering that phase was no small <u>occasion</u>.   _____

9. . . . living quarters provided for <u>seasonal</u> help   _____

10. . . . put them on the <u>soiled</u> mattress   _____

11. . . . after a <u>hasty</u> breakfast   _____

12. By <u>dusk</u> they'd made $80.   _____

APPLICATION

EXERCISE 12: Raising Preschool Children

Like Sam, preschool children are often placed in day care while their parents are at work. Many people think these children would be better off at home. However, other people think placing children in group day care is good for both children and their parents.

In this exercise, you are asked to think about Rita's situation as well as your own opinions about this issue. Write a short answer of one to four sentences in answer to each question.

1. Sam acts up when he has to go to the day-care center. What does he do to let Rita and his teachers know he isn't happy?

  a.

  b.

  c.

2. What are Rita's fears about Sam's behavior?

  a.

  b.

3. Rita would not necessarily have to go to work outside her home. She could continue to baby-sit at home, go on welfare, or try to get alimony and more child support from William.

  a. Why might having a job be important to Rita?

  b. List at least two arguments in favor of Rita's working outside her home.

  c. List at least two arguments against Rita's working outside her home.

  d. If you were Rita, what would you do? Why?

5. Now think about families you know who have preschool children. Think of two families whose children go to day care and two whose children are cared for at home by a parent.

a. What are the advantages of day care to the parent and children? What are the disadvantages?

b. What are the advantages of home care to the parent and children? What are the disadvantages?

ANSWERS ARE ON PAGES 182-83.

CHAPTER 6
Self-Discovery

SCENE 6
Bob and Carol

Carol had begun to treasure the few quiet hours at the end of the day. Bob would be home from the station, and their baby Evelyn would be asleep for the night. It was the only time she had to really relax. During the day, Evelyn often would sleep for no more than one hour at a time. In these brief moments Carol would clean, cook, do laundry, or sometimes take a short nap.

During her two years of nurse's training, Carol had constantly been around adults in the challenging environment of the hospital. Staying home with Evelyn, Carol missed the excitement and contact with other adults. In addition, she regretted not using her nurse's training.

Carol had not complained much about staying home, but she had been very depressed for some time. After having Evelyn, she had not bounced back physically. Instead of losing weight, she'd gained more. She was now thirty-five pounds heavier than when she had graduated from high school. At one point she had tried on one of her nurse's uniforms. Standing in front of the mirror, she remarked to herself that she looked like a great white whale.

Bob mentioned her weight problem to her, and she found herself unable to discuss it. Instead, she flew into a rage.

"Maybe I'm not cut out to be a mother," she told Bob. "I love the kid. I really don't mind the work of taking care of her, but there's something missing from my life. It drives me nuts to be here all day talking baby talk to her. . . . About the only contact I have with adults is watching the soaps on TV."

Bob was sympathetic, to a point. "What do you want to do about it?" he asked. "You could go back to work at the hospital, but you'd have to find a baby-sitter or day care for Evelyn."

Carol stared blankly at Bob for an instant. Without saying a word, she went into the bedroom and closed the door behind her. "I can't leave her with a baby-sitter, she thought. "She's too young . . . but I'm going to be a basket case if I don't." Then she began to think about how unfair life was. Bob could do what he wanted in his work while she was completely responsible for the baby.

Carol paced the floor of the bedroom for a moment. Then she stormed back to the living room to confront Bob. "Why is it that I have to be responsible for taking care of her or for finding a sitter?" she asked. Carol's body was trembling, but her words were controlled and cold. "Why shouldn't you be at least as responsible as me? After all, I've got an occupation, too. Why don't I work and you stay home?"

"Great," said Bob sarcastically. "We could share the misery." They sat for a moment saying nothing. Then, in a softer tone of voice, Bob said, "I can't just quit my job and stay home. I'm probably less cut out for that than you are. I would have gone nuts a long time ago."

"You're probably right about that, but it's still totally unfair that you get to work and I can't."

"But it'll just be for a year or two, until Eve is big enough to stay with a sitter."

"I just can't do it. It's more serious than you think. I cannot do this for a year."

Now Bob was becoming visibly angry. "It was your mistake that got you where

you are," he shouted. "You can't blame me because you didn't use the diaphragm."

"That's something we can't change. It's totally unfair of you to bring that up now. We would have had exactly the same problem even if we had waited to have kids. I am just not cut out to spend my life as a housewife."

"Then for your own good, you better figure out a way to get back to work. If things are that bad for you at home, you're not going to be happy. You'll be a miserable wife and a miserable mother!"

"Damn you!" shouted Carol. "How can you accuse me of not doing a good job with Evelyn when you do almost nothing with her yourself!"

"I didn't say that at all. I said if something doesn't change, you're going to be miserable. Up until now you must have been hiding all your unhappiness."

"Well, then maybe it would be better for Evelyn and me if I went back to work. . . . That's what I'll have to do. But what'll we do with Eve?"

Carol spent the better part of the following day writing and typing her resumé. When Bob got home from work they talked. "I do have to go back to work. . . . at least part-time," she said. "It's a relief to me just to think about it. I wrote a resumé today, and later this week I want to arrange interviews at the hospital and two clinics. Could you take care of Evelyn for a day when I go to interview?"

Bob agreed. On the day of the interview, he told Carol that he'd try to do the work she would have done. She should just leave him a list of things to do.

Taking care of the baby was not as easy as he'd hoped it would be. To Bob's dismay, he found that Evelyn required much more attention than he had thought. He started to do the laundry but had to respond to Evelyn's cry. He fed her and rocked her until she seemed to be asleep, and then he placed her in her crib. But the moment he got down to the basement to sort clothes, she began to cry again. Scenes like this repeated themselves throughout the day. When Carol came home, Bob was delighted to see her.

"How'd things go?" he asked.

"Oh geez, Bob," she said. "It was so nice to get out of the house, even for a day. . . . I had lunch with Andrea, the head nurse in the hospital emergency room, and she said that they have a half-time opening. How did you and Evelyn get along?"

"Just fine, but I'm real glad you're home."

"It looks like there are two jobs open," said Carol. "Besides the emergency room, I could work at the Anderson Clinic, but that's a full-time job. And do you know what? The hospital pays as much for half-time as the clinic pays for full-time. I would make $8,000 per year half-time at the hospital!"

"That's really neat, but what about Evelyn? What hours would you work?"

"It would be two days a week and then every other weekend. I was thinking that maybe my mother could take Evelyn during the week. You could take her on weekends."

"I suppose," said Bob. He sat down in a chair just as Evelyn began to cry in her room.

"I'll get her," said Carol. "By the way, what are we going to have for supper?"

"I haven't even thought about it," said Bob meekly.

Carol lost six pounds before her first day of work in the hospital emergency room. Within three months, she was the same weight she'd been when she graduated from high school. Her depression was gone.

"You were right," Bob told her. "It is better for both Evelyn and you if you work . . . and so it's better for me, too. You know, I've been thinking that I want a station of my own. That's going to take a lot of work. Let's look into that as our next project."

SCENE 2
Paul

Paul had never believed in banks. It wasn't because he thought that his money wouldn't be safe in a bank. The problem was that the bank could pass on information about him to the police or to the Internal Revenue Service. At times he had large sums of money, and he figured that a bank would become suspicious of anybody who made large and irregular cash deposits.

Paul still carried a large sum of "getaway money" in his wallet. But he didn't want to carry all his money with him because he could get mugged. So he'd put $400 in a cloth bag, moved a grate in his room, and hung the bag inside. Thinking that there could be a fire in the building, he had put another $400 behind the spare tire of his car.

He wondered what he'd do if he were rich. "How in the world could I spend the money and still stay underground?" he asked himself. It would be almost impossible to buy any real estate or even a new car. The government kept close track of such purchases to make sure that people were paying their sales and property taxes. Keeping a humble and inconspicuous life-style seemed to be the safest course of action, but this seemed less and less satisfying.

At first he'd been happy enough just to get away from the police. He found he could survive in a strange town on his own. But trying to be inconspicuous meant not having some of the things he'd eventually want. It also meant having few or no friends. He ate alone most of the time, and he'd seen almost every movie there was to see.

But loneliness and a poor standard of living were not his only problems. Certain incidents were causing him to seriously question his life-style and even his sanity. For example, he'd gone to a movie one afternoon. He'd parked his car a block from the theater and rushed to get to the movie on time. After the movie, he'd taken his time getting back to the car, only to discover that it was gone! "Maybe that's not where I left it," he thought to himself. He'd seen so many movies and parked in so many different places that they seemed to blend together. That made him uncertain about where he'd left the car.

He walked past the spot where he thought it had been. Then he walked around several of the blocks in the vicinity of the theater. As he walked, his mind began to reel with anger, then helplessness. Finally a sense of panic overtook him. Suddenly the features of every person he passed on the street seemed sinister and distorted. He had the overwhelming feeling that they were all after him. "Survival of the fittest," he thought. "The big fish eat the little fish." With that thought, he began to run back toward the spot where his car had been.

Once there, he saw that the sign at the curb said "No Parking 4–6 P.M." He looked at his watch and saw that it was past 4:30. "The cops have got it," he thought to himself. To make sure, he once again retraced his path to the theater and then walked back. The car was gone for sure.

He stopped and had a drink in a tavern across the street. Looking out on the street, he noticed that the curbs were full of trash, newspaper, and discarded cups and containers. The wind was blowing the trash, but not in any particular direction. The newspapers would take off as if they were going somewhere, but they'd circle around and then fall in about the same spot where they'd been. "That's life," he thought.

As Paul sipped his drink, he realized that he would not be able to get his car back. The risk was too great. At first this made him feel depressed. He'd lost the car and the $400 that was in the trunk.

Then it occurred to him that it really didn't matter. He still had as much money as he needed. For a brief moment he felt good again. But as he took the city bus back to his room, he slipped back into a state of depression. "I took so many risks to get the car and the money," he thought, "and for what, if it doesn't really matter?" It did matter a lot, he decided. But what mattered was not the car or the money. Rather, the whole incident left him with a hopeless feeling about his present and his future. "I've painted myself into a corner," he thought. "I've got nowhere to go and nothing to lose." He pushed his hand into the pocket that held his wallet and left it there as he looked at the faces of the people riding the bus. "I wouldn't trust any of them farther than I can spit," he thought.

Questions About the Story
MAIN IDEAS AND DETAILS

EXERCISE 1: Main Ideas and Supporting Evidence

Circle the letter of the choice that best completes each sentence. List at least one piece of evidence that supports your answer.

1. Carol is not satisfied staying home with Evelyn because
   a. she is gaining so much weight
   b. she is tired of watching soap operas on TV
   c. Bob won't stay home with them
   d. she wants to use her training and be with adults

   Evidence:

2. When Bob takes care of Evelyn while Carol goes on a job interview, he learns
   a. how to cook supper
   b. that he can do the laundry while Evelyn sleeps

   c.   that taking care of a baby is an easy job

   d.   that taking care of a baby is not an easy job

Evidence:

3.   Carol takes the half-time job in the emergency room because

   a.   the hours are better, though the pay is less

   b.   it is the only job offer she has

   c.   the hours are convenient and the pay is good

   d.   she wants to work full-time

Evidence:

4.   In the end, Bob decides that it is good for Carol to work because

   a.   Carol's mother can care for her grandchild

   b.   someday they want to have another child

   c.   Carol is much happier working

   d.   Bob wants a gas station of his own

Evidence:

5.   Paul does not use banks because

   a.   the bank might give information to the IRS

   b.   there are none in his neighborhood

   c.   he doesn't want to give anyone his address

   d.   he isn't afraid to carry his money with him

Evidence:

6.   Paul can never spend a lot of money because

   a.   his friends would wonder where he got it

   b.   he is perfectly happy with what he has

   c.   big spenders attract attention

   d.   there is more where it came from

Evidence:

7. Paul loses his car because

    a. someone steals it

    b. the police have it towed away

    c. he can't remember where he parked it

    d. someone wants the $400 in the trunk

Evidence:

EXERCISE 2: **True or False**

Indicate whether the following details are true (*T*) or false (*F*).

_____   **1.** Carol manages to lose a small amount of weight after having Evelyn.

_____   **2.** Carol thinks that it is unfair that she is totally responsible for caring for Evelyn.

_____   **3.** Bob has a hard day when he stays home to take care of Evelyn.

_____   **4.** Carol is tempted to take a job at the Anderson Clinic because it pays more.

_____   **5.** Paul is afraid that a bank would not give back his money.

_____   **6.** At first, Paul is not sure where he has left his car.

_____   **7.** Usually Paul eats with friends.

_____   **8.** Paul does not trust other people.

VOCABULARY

EXERCISE 3: **Synonyms and Antonyms**

> A **synonym** is a word or phrase that means the same or almost the same as another word or phrase. An **antonym** means the opposite. If you have trouble thinking of a synonym or antonym on your own, look up the word in a dictionary. You may get some ideas, or the dictionary may even give you a synonym.

Each phrase below contains an underlined word. In the blanks on the right, write a synonym and an antonym for the underlined word.

	Synonym	**Antonym**
1. Carol had begun to <u>treasure</u> the hours.	_____	_____
2. . . . <u>challenging</u> environment of the hospital	_____	_____

3. "Great," said Bob <u>sarcastically</u>. _____ _____

4. Her <u>depression</u> was gone. _____ _____

5. . . . living a <u>humble</u> life-style _____ _____

6. . . . features of every person seemed <u>sinister</u> _____ _____

APPLICATION
EXERCISE 4: Applying Your Values to Paul's Life

In a paragraph of three to four sentences, answer each of the following questions. Use a separate sheet of paper.

1. Paul, through his illegal activities, is making more money than any of the other characters in the story. Is he better or worse off than the other characters? Explain your answer.

2. Read over your answer to question 1. What values did you use to decide whether Paul is better or worse off? For example, if you value friendships highly, you may have said that Paul is worse off because he has no friends.

    List the values you used to answer question 1, and briefly explain why each is important to you.

3. Paul feels that the ruling principle of life is "survival of the fittest." In your own words, explain what he means by this phrase. To what extent do you agree with him?

ANSWERS ARE ON PAGE 183.

SCENE 3
Ted and Liz

It had been two years since Ted had first sailed with Liz and her parents. Now he and Liz had just taken the same trip but this time by themselves. The fact that they repeated it prompted Ted to look back on the two years that had passed. During the two years, he and Liz had been together steadily. Recently Liz had moved into his apartment.

Ted had continued to work for Liz's father and go to school. The biggest change in his life had been his relationship with Liz. He thought about what it meant to have been with Liz for two years, but it seemed impossible to know. He had no idea what his life would have been like without her. Rather, the memories of the two years raced through his mind in bits and pieces. Jogging together, taking a three-day bicycle trip, making love, cheering for her when she ran her first marathon, her crying on his shoulder when she felt she wasn't doing well enough in school, having Christmas with her parents, Liz giving him a haircut.

Ted admired Liz so much that he never even wondered why he loved her. But he often asked himself whether Liz really needed him. Liz was beautiful, rich, and full of life. Ted had always felt that she could have had any man she wanted. So, he wondered, why had she chosen him? And what would become of them?

Liz was to graduate from the University after the fall semester. She'd worked hard and had completed a four-year degree in just three and a half years. Ted, on the other hand, had continued in school but always on a part-time basis. He would not get a degree for two or two and a half more years.

During their last year in college, most students applied for work through the University's job placement service. Though Liz was not at all sure what she wanted to do, she had put her resumé on file and had interviewed for several jobs.

Companies came to the University from all over the country to interview graduating students. If they were impressed with a student, they'd invite the student to the company's home office for a second interview. Liz had already been invited for second interviews by two companies. One had paid her way to Houston, Texas, and the other to Minneapolis, Minnesota.

It scared Ted to think that Liz might accept a job halfway across the country. But both times when Liz returned from her trips, she had already decided that she did not want the jobs.

"It was really a strange experience," she told Ted. "I was applying for the job, so of course I was trying to impress them. But at the same time, they had already paid my expenses. So it was clear they were serious about me and were trying to impress me. At times we seemed to be falling all over each other trying to be pleasant and interesting."

"I think I'm jealous," Ted said. "Nobody's coming to me with job offers."

"How in the world could you be jealous, Ted? I don't really want either of the jobs, so what's there to be jealous of? . . . At least you've got a job that you like. I should really be jealous of you!"

"To be honest with you, those jobs you turned down looked pretty good to me. What is it you want in a job?"

"I don't know. I know I'd like to do something that's important. And by that I mean important because it helps people. The two companies I interviewed with kept talking about how much money they were making and how much I might make. They didn't sound like they cared about anything else."

"What do you mean?"

"They should have concern for the people who buy their products."

"Look, Liz, they make a product, and they put it on the market. Nobody is forced to buy what they make. Anyone can take it or leave it. So those people who buy from them must be getting what they want, or they wouldn't buy. What more can they do than give people what they want?"

"Hey, come on! The answer isn't that simple. What if a person wanted something that was bad for him? Let's say you're a bartender. You've got a drunk at the bar who's going to drive home in a few minutes, and he orders another drink. According to your little formula, you'd give him another drink because that's what he wants, and 'What more can you do than give people what they want?' "

"Well, I wouldn't give him the drink."

"I didn't think you would, and you know why? Because you've got a sense of social responsibility. You'd think about the drunk killing himself or someone else because of that extra drink. And you'd tell him to forget it. So you don't really believe in just giving people what they want. You'd also make judgments about the effect it would have."

"I see what you mean. But if you expect too much from your work, you're going to get in a real bind. Where in the world are you going to find a job where the main ingredient is caring about people?"

"Well . . . I talked to a recruiter for the Peace Corps last week. It looks like I could get in. . . . We talked about my working in a Spanish-speaking country, probably in South America."

"Oh God," said Ted. "Would you really do that? Would you go to South America?"

"It's something that I have to get out of my system, Ted. I know how idealistic that must sound to you."

"But what about us? You just moved in, and now you're talking about moving out."

"I'd sign up for two years. That isn't so long. It's something that I couldn't do later."

"Two years! Two years can be a hell of a long time! I've only known you for two years, and it seems like forever. I can't imagine you being gone that long."

"It would be hard for me too. I'd miss you a lot," she said as she reached out to hug Ted.

As she reached for him, Ted grabbed both of her hands and rigidly held her away. "Don't talk to me about leaving for two years one minute and then try to get close the next minute," he said. "I thought we really had something going. If you really cared for me, you'd stay right here. I thought you cared."

Liz eased her hands out of Ted's grip and backed away from him.

"I wanted to be reasonable about this," she said, "but you're pushing me into a corner. We're only twenty-one years old, and when I get back we'll only be twenty-three. We'll have the rest of our lives to do whatever we want."

"You're so wrapped up in yourself you don't even think about me," said Ted. He lay down on the sofa and buried his face in a pillow. Liz sat beside him for a moment not touching him.

"I don't see how you can say that I only care about myself," she said. "When we started this conversation, I was telling you that I want to help other people."

"So you want to run off and help people you don't even know."

"They need help," she said. "You're doing just fine, and you'll do fine without me. . . . It's really not that long." She put her hand on Ted's shoulder as if to turn him over to face her. Ted twisted violently on the couch, pushing Liz's hand away. "Go away," he said.

Liz did leave the apartment. She returned the next day, but Ted wouldn't talk to her. Soon after she'd arrived, he left without saying a word. The same scene was repeated the following day, and this time Liz packed up most of her belongings. She left the following note:

> Dear Ted,
>   I'm sorry that we haven't been able to work things out. I have moved back to my parents' house, and I'll be there for the next three weeks. Then I'll be going to a training center in Florida for thirteen weeks.
>   I hope you understand that this is very important to me. I feel that I must do it. I would like to write to you while I'm away, and I do regret the effect that this decision is having on our relationship. I am hoping to hear from you soon.
>   Love,
>   Liz

Ted did not contact Liz before she left. He was hurt and angry. "Let her go," he kept telling himself. "What good is she if she's not loyal?"

Questions About the Story
MAIN IDEAS AND DETAILS

EXERCISE 5: Locating Supporting Details

Find details in the reading that support each of the following main ideas.

1. Ted recalls a lot of memorable moments with Liz. List several of his memories.

   a.

   b.

   c.

   d.

2. Ted admires Liz very much. List three outstanding characteristics that Ted sees in Liz.

   a.

   b.

   c.

3. Liz is determined to go into the Peace Corps, no matter what effect her decision has on Ted.

   a.

b.

c.

EXERCISE 6: Summarizing Essential Information

Summarizing means picking out only the essential information and getting a point across in as few words as possible. For example, you could summarize Liz's note to Ted on page 132 like this:

1. Pick out the essential facts and ideas in the note.

- Liz is leaving soon
- she is sorry that her relationship with Ted has fallen apart and hopes to talk to him
- going into the Peace Corps is very important to Liz

2. Using these essential facts and ideas, write a sentence or two that summarizes the note.

I'm leaving soon, and it's very important for me to go. I want to talk to you before I go because I'm sorry things are bad between us.

Write a sentence or two to summarize the following events and ideas from the story. Be sure to pick out the essential facts before you write your summary.

1. Summarize the process Liz goes through when she uses the University's job placement service.

2. Summarize what Liz wants to get out of a job.

3. Summarize the reasons Liz wants to join the Peace Corps.

READING BETWEEN THE LINES

EXERCISE 7: A Characterization of Ted

This exercise asks you to study Ted. He is a somewhat contradictory character—in some ways he is mature and responsible, but he is also capable of acting childishly. You may need to refer to scenes about Ted in earlier chapters to answer these questions.

Write at least one sentence in response to each question. Use a separate sheet of paper.

1. What does Ted's success at the McKenna Company tell you about him?

2. In Ted's job and in his relationship with Liz, is Ted a leader or a follower? Support your answer with examples.

3. What does Ted's response to Liz's question about the drunk reveal about his values?

4. What does Ted's response to Liz's plans reveal about his personality or his character?

5. What do you think is most important to Ted? Cite at least two pieces of evidence for your answer.

6. Below is a list of values. For each one, write at least one sentence in which you compare and contrast (look for similarities and differences in) what each means to Ted and what each means to Liz.

    a. ambition

    b. security

    c. loyalty

    d. prosperity

    d. independence

APPLICATION

EXERCISE 8: Clarifying Your Own Values

Now consider what each of the five values above means to you. Write a sentence or two about each one. Use a separate sheet of paper.

1. ambition

2. security

3. loyalty

4. prosperity

5. independence

ANSWERS ARE ON PAGE 183.

SCENE 4
Rita

As Rita's success in police work increased, she found that she had higher expectations for her personal life. She had passed the GED and was about to graduate from the police academy. In addition, through the physical training, Rita's feelings about her body and appearance had changed. While she had always considered herself smart and attractive, she now began to approach the world with far more confidence.

During her separation from William, a number of men had asked her out. Each time she had refused. She couldn't handle another relationship yet, she had told herself. But that feeling changed over time, partly as a result of Rita's new confidence.

The police academy brought in a number of visiting experts to instruct the trainees. One of the last visiting teachers came in from another state to do a ten-day course on crime detection. Rita entered the classroom as she had for the past sixteen weeks, thinking about her schoolwork and about her afternoon assignment to work the central city beat. The visiting instructor was at the front of the room, putting his exhibits in order for the class. He looked up and began to take notice of the trainees. Rita, who was sitting toward the back of the room, was immediately impressed. He had the build of a career cop who had made staying in top shape part of his job. His face was rugged and handsome in spite of a narrow, half moon-shaped scar on his forehead.

As Rita studied him, their eyes met. He put down his papers and walked directly to the back of the room.

"Do we know each other?" he asked Rita.

"Not yet," she said and looked down at the table.

"Too forward," she thought to herself. "He's going to think I'm easy."

"I'm Josh Martin," he said, starting to smile. "I don't mean to be too forward, but I thought I knew you from somewhere else."

"It's OK," said Rita. "But I don't think we've met. I'm Rita Ahlgetti." His handshake was firm and warm.

"I see that you're going to be doing a ten-day class. . . ."

Josh nodded and smiled again. "You keep awake," he said, ". . . because, baby, I'm gonna be calling on you."

Rita smiled back. "Fine," she said. "I'll be ready. . . . By the way, only my mama calls me baby. You can call me Officer Ahlgetti in class and Rita if we should meet on the street." Josh laughed an easy laugh and turned to walk back to the front of the room.

On the second day of class, Josh joined Rita and some of the other trainees in the cafeteria for lunch. Rita was finding him to be a good instructor as well as a very attractive man. They lingered after lunch and were the last two people sitting at the table.

"It gets lonely traveling around to give this dog and pony show. How about going out for a bite later this afternoon?"

Out of habit, Rita started to say no. "I've got to pick up my boy," she said. "I don't think. . ." She stopped and looked at Josh.

"That's OK," he said. "You decide. . . . We could pick up your boy and take him along."

"Yes," said Rita. "Yeah, let's go out. It's time."

"It's what?"

"I said, 'it's time,' but I have to get down to the squad room. I can explain later. . . . I'll be back at the dispatcher's office at four-thirty. See you there?"

"See you there, Rita."

"What you meant to say was, 'See you there, Officer Ahlgetti,' " Rita said, smiling and walking toward the squad room.

At the end of the day, Rita changed into street clothes at the station, and she and Josh picked up Sam. They decided to buy a bottle of wine and sandwiches and have supper at a park. "You're not a cop," Sam said to Josh. "You haven't got a uniform or a gun."

"Some cops dress just like people," Josh said, "and I've got no use for a gun. I'm a teacher now."

"That's OK," said Sam. "Not everybody can be a real cop like Mama."

Josh laughed and picked up Sam, placing him on the branch of an overhanging tree that was about six feet off the ground. Sam struggled and complained but then seemed not to mind his perch. "You come help me down," he demanded.

"Not till you say I'm a cop."

"You don't have a gun."

"You're going to be up in that tree for a long time."

"Mama, help!"

"I can't reach," said Rita. "You're going to have to get help from Officer Martin."

"He really a cop?" Sam asked.

"That's good enough," said Josh, hauling Sam out of the tree. "You said it."

"I was just asking," said Sam. "You put me back up there."

"No way," said Josh. "You might get stubborn and ruin the picnic."

"They'll get along just fine," Rita thought.

On his fourth night in town, Rita invited Josh to her apartment for dinner. Sam would be with William, and for the first time, Rita and Josh would be alone. Rita tried to time everything so that William would pick up Sam before Josh arrived. But William was late and arrived after Josh.

"Whose car?" he asked Rita, pointing at Josh's rented car.

"I have a friend over," she replied.

"I'm comin' in for a minute," William said, pushing by Rita. "Where's Sam?"

"Out back with the neighbor kids," said Rita.

"You got a man?" William entered the hall and looked into the living room where Josh was sitting.

"You seein' my woman?" he asked Josh. Rita could tell that William had been drinking.

William walked over to Josh. Josh stood and held out his hand. "Josh Martin," he said, introducing himself. William slapped at the hand. "I assume that was a handshake," said Josh.

.

"You're late, William," Rita said.

William aimed a kick at Rita, missed, and tried to slap her on the side of the head. She stopped the slap in midair and was thinking of using her police training when Josh got up from the sofa.

"Lay off," he said, grabbing William's arm and trying to lead him outside. William threw a punch at Josh, but Josh turned him and sent him sprawling on the ground. William got up and came toward Josh, swinging. Josh went into a boxer's stance and hit William with a right. William lay spread-eagled, out cold, on the floor of the hallway leading to Rita's apartment.

"I'm sorry," said Josh.

"It's OK," gasped Rita. "He had it coming."

"I know that," said Josh. "I'm not sorry about hitting the man. I just wish I'd let you take care of him."

The two went inside the apartment and locked the door.

"You think we better call the police?" asked Josh.

"I'd be too embarrassed. . . . I know so many of them," said Rita. She started to laugh, a little hysterically.

They looked back out into the hallway and found that William had disappeared. "I think he's had enough police action for one day," said Rita. "Let's get Sam to bed and have that supper I promised you."

When Sam woke up the following morning, he found Josh sleeping on the sofa. He said nothing but turned on the cartoons on TV. When Josh woke up, Sam watched him out of the corner of his eye but was silent. "Mornin', Sam," Josh ventured. Sam remained silent.

Finally Sam spoke. "You beat up my dad," he said.

"Sorry," said Josh slowly.

Sam turned back to the cartoon and was silent again. Josh watched him for several minutes. Then he picked up the small boy and held him until Rita came downstairs to make breakfast.

Josh stayed for the weekend and returned to stay again the night before he left town. "I'll call you," he told Rita when it was time to leave. "I'll be passing this way again. . . . I'll see you."

SCENE 5
Djuan

With a little coaxing from Djuan, the manager of the farm set a time when they could work on Djuan's car. They'd tear down the engine on a Sunday afternoon, get the parts they needed before going to the fields on Monday, and reassemble the engine in the next few evenings.

"You might as well do most of the work," the manager had said, " 'cause you'll learn more that way."

"Don't know if I can," Djuan said. Deep down, he wondered if the manager was really going to honor his promise to fix Djuan's car. Djuan imagined how hard it would be for them if he could not get the car back together and they were stuck out on a northern Florida farm with no transportation.

In spite of his fears, he walked down the road to the manager's house on Sunday afternoon and got the tools needed to take apart the engine. He carefully removed the assemblies from on top of the engine: carburetor, linkage, valve covers, and valve lifters. As these pieces were removed, Djuan placed them next to the car in the order that he had removed them. As he took nuts and bolts off, he lightly turned them back into the threaded seats that they had come out of. That, he thought, was the only way he could possibly remember how to reassemble the engine.

After supper, Djuan jacked up the car and placed blocks under the frame. Then he began to take apart the engine from the bottom, removing the oil pan and then the crankshaft bearings. The manager appeared carrying a small toolbox.

"You really been goin' at it," the manager said. "We can be done takin' 'er apart before it's dark."

The manager sat beside the car as Djuan handed him pieces from underneath. "We'll take some bearings and the crankshaft and piston into town tomorrow," he said. "They got a shop manual at the store, so we'll borrow it. . . . Then you gotta measure your pieces to see if they're in tolerance or if you need new ones. You're gonna need money."

Djuan had trouble sleeping that night. Being out on a farm and far from home with no means of transportation made him insecure. What if someone in the family had a medical problem and needed to go to the hospital?

Then his thoughts turned to his first wife. The familiar scene came back into his mind. . . . She walks up behind the large truck full of workers as Djuan stands on the bed of the truck looking down at her. She extends her hand to Djuan, silently asking him to help her up onto the truck. At that moment, her face in all its beauty and life pleads for a small favor, a helping hand after a hard day's work. In Djuan's memory the face now pleaded again. But in this scene his hand and arms don't move. They remain at his side—until the truck lurches.

He had asked himself a thousand times why he couldn't reach over the gate of the truck. Was she asking too much? After lifting thousands of pounds of vegetables in a day, didn't she deserve a small lift herself? Even if she had done no work, she was his wife and was asking for a favor that could have been accomplished in an instant. Djuan said a short prayer, then he buried his head into his pillow and tried to sleep. He'd feel better when the car was running again.

The next day, the manager taught Djuan to measure and evaluate the car's old parts. They had to buy $170 in new parts. Working after a day in the fields until very late, Djuan and the manager completed the underside of the engine on Monday. On Wednesday, they finished the top of the engine. Then Djuan turned the key in the ignition, and to his delight the engine came to life.

"Look, no smoke!" the manager yelled.

Tessa and Marissa came out of the house applauding. They rushed up to Djuan and hugged him as he got out of the car and walked to the back to look at the exhaust. Yulanda, holding Carlo, looked out of the door of the living quarters. She beamed, and Carlo let out a big belly laugh.

"You did it," Tessa and Marissa shouted. "You fixed it so it runs good!"

"Purrs like a kitten," the manager said. "She ought to last for a long time."

Djuan threw his hands up in triumph and then patted the top of the old car, waving to Yulanda as he got in to take it for a test drive.

Later he talked about how good it felt when he heard the engine start. "I just couldn't believe that I'd done something that hard...got all the pieces fit back so it would run." He laughed and chased the children around the living quarters until they were tired.

"How about ice cream?" asked Marissa.

"Ice cream!" yelled Djuan. "To town. We go to town and get big sundaes. We'll take the new car!"

Questions About the Story
MAIN IDEAS AND DETAILS
EXERCISE 9: Supporting Evidence for Inferred Main Ideas

Main ideas are not always directly stated. Sometimes you have to piece together events and things people think or say to discover ideas that are implied. When you do this, you are **inferring main ideas**.

List at least one piece of evidence to support each inferred main idea.

1. Rita is ready to go out with men.
   Evidence:

2. Rita wants Josh to respect her.
   Evidence:

3. Josh is good at dealing with Sam.
   Evidence:

4. Rita is no longer afraid of William.
   Evidence:

5. Djuan is afraid the car's engine will never be put back together again.
   Evidence:

6. Djuan still feels some strong emotions about his first wife.

Evidence:

7. Djuan and his family take great pride in his fixing the car.

Evidence:

EXERCISE 10: Sequence

Number the following events in the order they occurred in the lives of the characters.

Rita

_____   **a.** Josh came to Rita's for dinner.

_____   **b.** Josh sat down at Rita's table for lunch.

_____   **c.** Josh and Rita bought wine and sandwiches.

_____   **d.** Josh asked Rita out for a bite.

_____   **e.** William came to pick up Sam.

_____   **f.** William tried to slap Rita.

Djuan

_____   **a.** Djuan threw up his hands in triumph.

_____   **b.** The engine was put back together.

_____   **c.** Djuan and the manager went to town for parts.

_____   **d.** The whole family went to town.

_____   **e.** The manager started helping Djuan fix the car.

_____   **f.** Djuan started the engine.

_____   **g.** Djuan thought about his first wife.

APPLICATION

EXERCISE 11: Competence

Rita and Djuan are both developing a greater sense of their own competence. Becoming more competent is, in fact, an important theme in this book. This assignment asks you to investigate this theme. Use a separate sheet of paper.

1. Write a definition of _competence_ in your own words. Then look it up in the dictionary.

2. Becoming more competent may affect both how a person sees himself or herself and how the person is viewed by others.

List at least two ways that being more competent has affected each of the following characters throughout the book:

Rita

Djuan

Ted

Carol

3. Based on the story, explain in a paragraph of three to four sentences how becoming more competent affects how people feel about themselves.

4. Now examine your own life. When have you felt that you were becoming more competent? How did your new competence affect your life? Why did it produce those effects?

Write a letter to a friend of two paragraphs or more to answer these questions. Use at least two examples from your own life.

ANSWERS ARE ON PAGES 183-84.

CHAPTER 7
Scenes of Resolution

SCENE 1
Djuan

Djuan awoke in the darkness of the living quarters and looked at the alarm clock. It was just after four o'clock, and he'd awakened because he was cold. The summer was almost over, and a late August thunderstorm had sent the nighttime temperature into the low sixties. Djuan covered Yulanda and pulled the other half of the blanket up around his neck. Yulanda rolled over and pushed against Djuan to keep warm. Djuan smiled to himself as he felt the baby move inside her.

The change in the weather and the late stages of Yulanda's pregnancy signaled that it was nearly time for the family to head north, toward home. All things considered, Djuan thought it had been a very good summer. In July, the manager had laid off all the other workers but had kept Djuan and his family. They'd done planting for the second crop, and Djuan and the manager had worked nights repairing other pieces of equipment.

Djuan had not expected that they'd work at the same farm all summer, but when the opportunity arose, they stayed in one place. "You're a damn good worker," the manager told Djuan. "You're not afraid of work. And you're smart. . . . Not many people can help with the machines."

He'd asked Djuan if they could stay on into the fall to finish the second harvest. The manager's offer was tempting. The cigar box was nearly full, and at last count it had contained over $3,600. "I could start filling a second cigar box," Djuan thought. But then he remembered his promise to take Yulanda home before the baby was born. He also felt strongly that Marissa and Tessa would be better off going to school at home with their friends.

As he lay in the silence of the morning, Djuan became aware of the sound of his children's breathing. All three could be heard because the entire family slept in the same room, separated only by a short partition. Usually he was not aware of the sound of the children sleeping, but this morning the sound was different. Djuan detected one breathing harder and faster than the rest.

He got up quietly and moved slowly over to the other side of the partition. There he could tell that Marissa was having trouble. He bent down and touched her forehead. She was sweating, and her pillow and sheet were soaked. Kneeling next to her, Djuan could hear a raspy sound.

"You OK, Marissa?" he asked.

When she did not answer, Djuan pushed at her arm, coaxing her to wake up. Finally she awoke enough to begin talking, but she seemed to be having a nightmare. Tessa and Yulanda awoke and joined Djuan.

"She's having a bad dream," Djuan said.

"Yes, but she has fever too," said Yulanda, ". . . pretty sick girl."

They gave Marissa aspirin, and Yulanda changed the pillowcase and carefully washed Marissa's face and shoulders with cool water.

"Maybe we need to take her to a doctor," Tessa said.

"If she's no better by morning, we'll take her to the hospital," Djuan replied.

Djuan and Yulanda returned to their bed, but neither could sleep. Each lay awake listening to Marissa's breathing, which seemed to get increasingly hoarse and raspy. By morning there was no improvement. Marissa did not fully awaken, but seemed to be living through one bad dream after another.

Yulanda held Marissa as Djuan drove to the hospital. After checking Marissa's heart and breathing, the nurse looked quite concerned.

"She has a high fever," she said "and her breathing is difficult. . . . Can you wait outside while I have the doctor examine her?"

Djuan crossed his fingers for good luck and prayed silently to himself as he and Yulanda moved to the waiting room. A hospital secretary approached Djuan and asked how he wished to pay the hospital fee. He'd pay with cash, Djuan said, thinking of the cigar box full of money in the trunk of the car.

After some time, the nurse returned.

"We've started a number of tests," she said. "We've got to wait for the results before we have much of an idea about what's causing the problem. . . . It looks like a case of pneumonia."

Later, when the tests were completed, the nurse asked Djuan and Yulanda to step back into the room where Marissa was being examined.

"About Marissa," the doctor started, ". . . there's just no way to tell what's wrong. She looks like she's got pneumonia, but the blood tests say that she doesn't. I'd like to admit her to the hospital for today and tonight so we can keep a close eye on her."

"Yes, yes." Djuan said. He stared at Marissa, who was sleeping. Then he turned to the doctor, looking directly into his eyes. "Can you make her well?" Djuan asked.

The doctor appeared to be startled by the directness of Djuan's gaze and question.

"I think so," he said, but as he replied, he turned his eyes away from Djuan's and looked blankly at the floor.

Djuan grabbed the doctor by the arms, forcing the taller man to look directly at him.

"You must make her well," he told the doctor. "Nothing in the world is as important as making Marissa better."

"I understand," the doctor began. "But . . ."

"No! No buts," Djuan interrupted. "No excuses . . . you make her better."

"OK," the doctor replied.

By the next morning, Marissa's fever had gone down slightly, and her breathing sounded normal.

"We still don't know the cause," the doctor said. "It could be a virus, or it could be a reaction to a mold or something she breathed. We just can't tell."

The doctor went on to say that he'd recommend releasing Marissa, but that she should be returned immediately to a hospital if her fever went up or if she had any trouble breathing.

One night in the hospital, including tests and doctors' fees, came to $496. Djuan paid the bill with money from the cigar box.

"I don't trust this hospital," Djuan told Yulanda on the way back to the farm. "I wish we were home where our own doctor could see her."

"We must go soon anyway," she replied. "Soon I will need my doctor. . . . Maybe we go today or tomorrow."

Djuan thought for a moment.

"If her fever got worse on the way home, we could stop at another hospital. Any hospital on the way would probably be as good as this one. . . . We'll start home today."

While Marissa rested, they packed the car. Djuan told the farm manager why they suddenly had to leave.

"You come back anytime you need work," the manager said as the family left.

Djuan drove north, and Tessa held Carlo in the front seat. In the back seat, Yulanda cared for Marissa, trying to keep her as comfortable as possible on the journey home.

During the first twelve hours of driving, there was no change in Marissa's condition. By the time they were halfway home Djuan was very tired, and they decided to check into a motel to eat and sleep. On the following day there still seemed to be no change for the worse in Marissa's condition, so again they drove north.

Late that day, as it began to get dark, Tessa and Carlo lay curled up in the front seat sleeping. Yulanda, reaching from the back seat, touched Djuan's shoulder.

"Marissa is starting to sweat," she said. "I think her fever gets worse."

Djuan pulled over to the side of the road and got out to check on Marissa.

"I'm OK, Papa," Marissa said, but Djuan could tell that Yulanda was right. The fever was getting worse.

As Djuan got back in the driver's seat, he figured out how far they were from home.

"One hundred and sixty miles to go," he thought. "Yulanda," he said, ". . . we're about three hours from home. I think we'll try to make it."

"If she gets worse, we better stop."

"I'm OK, Papa . . . I'm OK, Papa," Marissa repeated.

"Marissa doesn't even know what she's saying," Djuan thought to himself. He pushed the car's accelerator down and held the speed at seventy-five miles per hour. "If I don't get caught by the police, we'll be home in about two hours," he thought.

As the old car raced toward home, the whole family thought about Marissa. Even when she was terribly sick and only half conscious, she didn't want to be a burden.

"I'm OK, Papa," she kept repeating as they raced through the darkness.

SCENE 2
Bob

Bob had expected that the first months of owning his own gas station would be the most difficult. He'd painted the outside of the station and scrubbed and painted the shop floor. The tools that he had purchased were clean and carefully arranged. On the day before the station opened, he'd strung up colorful pennants around the outside. That night he stayed up late, carefully painting a sign that said "Station Under New Management."

On the morning that the station opened, Carol and Evelyn went to the station with Bob to help him celebrate. By seven-thirty Bob had introduced himself to his first customer. After taking the man's money, he walked proudly back to the station, waving the first dollar that he'd earned in his own business. Carol and Evelyn cheered and clapped. They immediately put the dollar into a frame and hung it on the wall behind the cash register.

But as the morning wore on, it was clear that customers were not going to flock to the station in great numbers. Bob and his mechanic spent much of the day just talking and occasionally pumping gas for customers who strayed in. At the end of the day, Bob tallied his receipts and made a mental note of how well he'd done. He'd worked eleven hours and had not even made enough profit to pay his mechanic.

The next day was the same as the first. By the end of the week, Bob realized that he'd spent almost fifty hours at the station and had nothing to show for his time and energy. Over the weekend, he decided he'd try advertising as a way to bring in more customers. He could advertise in the newspaper, but that was expensive. It was also not a good way to attract customers from the immediate neighborhood. "Why don't you go door to door?" Carol asked. "At least that wouldn't cost you anything except some more time."

"What would I say?" Bob asked.

"You could just introduce yourself and say that you want their business," Carol replied.

Bob thought he'd feel better about doing that if he had something special to offer people, so he decided on a very inexpensive "oil change special." He would make almost no money on the oil changes, but at least he'd be able to meet his potential customers. That evening, Bob carefully drew up a leaflet advertising the special, had it copied, and started taking it from house to house.

Slowly business began to pick up, but it wasn't until the seventh week that Bob

made any profit for himself.

"Seven weeks of work," he thought, "and I've got $34 to show for my trouble. . . . So far I've made less than 10¢ per hour."

He decided to keep the station open until 10:00 P.M., hoping that customers would come in after supper. At first he stayed until 10:00 himself, but Carol complained that she and Evelyn never saw him. So Bob placed an advertisement in the help-wanted section of the newspaper in search of a person to work the evening shift.

A young man by the name of Jerry Rafsky was one of the first to respond.

"Are you any relation to Paul Rafsky?" Bob asked.

"He's my older brother," Jerry replied.

"God, I haven't thought about Paul for months," Bob said. "How's he doing?"

"Nobody knows," said Jerry. "Haven't heard."

"He was my friend. You could trust me not to say anything if you've heard from him," Bob said.

"No kidding. No, I was being straight with you. He just seemed to disappear into thin air. As far as I know the cops aren't even looking for him anymore, but nobody knows how to get in touch with him."

"Well, look, kid . . . for old time's sake I'm going to put you on. You won't be doing any mechanical work, you'll just be pumping gas."

Jerry quickly learned to run the station by himself in the evenings. The gas receipts were enough to pay for Jerry's wages and provide a small margin of profit. Bob grew to like him, partly because he saw some of Paul's spirit of independence in him.

"But Paul was never willing to work," Bob thought. "Maybe if I keep Jerry going here, he won't turn out the same way Paul did."

By the fifth month, business had picked up to the point that Bob could show a small but growing profit, at least on paper. He had not, however, taken any of the profits for himself. He and Carol lived on Carol's salary, and all the money that Bob made he put back into the station by increasing his inventory of tools and supplies.

After six months, Bob decided that it was time to do a very careful inventory to determine his actual profit. Along with his bookkeeper, he had established an accounting system that allowed him to know exactly how much inventory he should have on hand. In fact, the system worked so well that when Bob did the inventory, he became certain that he'd lost almost $2,000 in supplies.

"I just don't understand it," Bob told the bookkeeper. "When we sell something, it goes onto the tape, and you take the figures right off the tape. The only way this could have happened is if things were sold but not rung up on the cash register."

"You've got it," said the accountant. "And there's only two possibilities. "Either someone comes in at night and steals the inventory, or it's an inside job."

Bob guessed immediately that Jerry had been stealing from him.

"What's missing?" he asked the accountant.

"Looks like tires, batteries, and oil . . . at least two dozen tires, six batteries, several cases of oil, and then some odds and ends."

That evening Bob confronted Jerry.

"I found out today that we're missing almost $2,000 in inventory," Bob told him. "That's more than my entire profit for a half year's work. . . ." He looked carefully at Jerry, trying to gauge his reaction.

Jerry looked away momentarily and then began to talk fast.

"I didn't do nothin' . . ." he stammered; ". . . don't know nothin' about it. Don't you try to pin that rap on me. . . . You got no proof I did nothin'. . . . I'll just quit."

"Look, Jerry . . . I haven't accused you of anything," said Bob.

"I'm on my way," said Jerry. "I'm not workin' anyplace where they suddenly accuse you of stealin' . . . and you said you were a friend of Paul's."

"How else could we have lost the inventory?" Bob asked, but Jerry was already walking toward his car. "I should nail the little turkey," Bob thought to himself. But instead he walked back into the station and stood motionlessly while Jerry drove away. Then Bob turned and hammered his fist against the wall of the station . . . again and again . . . until he saw that the paint was becoming pink from the raw spots on his knuckles.

SCENE 3
Carol

Carol looked up from the counter as the headlights of a vehicle rapidly approached the door to the emergency room. At first she thought it was an ambulance arriving, but she couldn't recall any ambulance calling in to say a patient was on the way.

As the vehicle turned and came into view, Carol could see that it wasn't an ambulance. Rather, it was an older sedan. The car screeched to a stop, and a man got out of the driver's seat. He ran around the car and hurriedly opened the door on the passenger side. A crying woman got out of the car, and then the two people reached in and pulled out the motionless body of a young girl.

"Get the cart," Carol yelled to the orderly in the next room. She ran to the door to assist the man and the woman.

"What happened?" she asked.

"We thought it wasn't so bad," the man said. He was cradling the limp girl in his arms. "She seemed to be doing fine, but on the way here she stopped breathing. We thought it would take too long to call. . . ."

"Get the cart out here!" Carol screamed at the orderly behind her. "And give us a Dr. Bluecart on the page!" Controlling her voice, she turned again to the man. "Put her down softly," she said.

"On the concrete?"

"Right now. On the concrete."

Carol knelt over the girl for only an instant before she began mouth-to-mouth breathing. At the same time, her fingers moved back and forth across the girl's neck, searching for a pulse. Finding no sign of a heartbeat, Carol raised herself up and began to push rhythmically on the girl's chest with both hands.

Behind her she heard the paging system calling for Dr. Bluecart to come immediately to the emergency room, and she knew that momentarily a team of doctors and nurses would be there to help her. She knelt down again and breathed into the young girl. An orderly rammed a cart through the swinging doors to the emergency room.

"Get the oxygen ready," gasped Carol.

The girl's parents had stepped back as the cart and hospital personnel began to arrive on the scene. The girl's mother was hysterical. The father was standing helplessly at her side, saying over and over, "We should have called an ambulance. . . . I told you we should have called an ambulance."

"We're ready," said a doctor behind Carol. Others lifted the girl onto the cart as Carol continued to breathe for her. When he was ready with the oxygen, the doctor nudged Carol away from the girl's mouth and began inserting a tube into the girl's throat. Carol rose and gave several pumps on the girl's chest. Once the tube was in place, the doctor yelled "OK, let's go," and the group surrounding the cart moved like an animal with twelve feet into the critical care area.

Though there were no signs of life from the motionless girl, they worked for nearly two hours as if she would be brought back to life at any moment. But then one of the doctors said what nobody in the room had been willing to consider: "It's all over. We've lost her."

Carol burst into tears and began to cry uncontrollably. She sat down in a chair at the edge of the room. This was not the first time that she'd lost a patient, and it wouldn't be the last.

"Damn!" she said to nobody in particular. "Why does this have to happen?"

"We did everything we could," one of the doctors said to her.

"Oh God, I know we did," Carol sobbed. "But why did it happen to someone so young . . . and with so much life left?"

"You going to be all right?" the doctor asked.

"Of course," Carol said.

"Will you tell the parents?" he asked.

"Yes," she said, "if I can just stop crying."

Meanwhile, thirty miles south of the hospital where Carol worked, Djuan was passing a line of cars. He was doing a steady eighty miles per hour.

"She's starting to have trouble breathing," Yulanda said from the back seat.

"Nothing to do but drive and pray," Djuan said. "I'm going to stay on the interstate and get her to University Hospital."

Three miles from the exit that led to the hospital, Djuan passed a police car parked underneath a bridge. Looking at her radar scope, Rita almost couldn't believe her eyes.

"Geezus," she said. "We've got someone here doing almost ninety miles per hour and heading right downtown. We may not be able to catch this one." She turned on her red top lights and siren and radioed ahead, telling other squad cars to be on the lookout for a fast-moving sedan. Then she floored the accelerator, squealing her tires as she lit out after Djuan.

Djuan saw the police car approaching, but it was still a half mile away. It would take too long to stop and explain, he thought, and he pushed on. As he approached the exit to the hospital, the squad car was getting close. Now he could hear the siren. He swerved onto a city street, slowing to fifty miles per hour. The squad car stayed right on his tail as he sped into the hospital's emergency entrance.

Just as the parents of the dead girl left the emergency room, Carol heard sirens outside the entrance.

"What now?" she asked the clerk.

"No ambulances have called in," the clerk replied.

"Another surprise," Carol thought as she ran through the entrance toward the flashing lights. The police car with the flashing lights was parked behind an older car, and the policewoman was already in the back seat doing mouth-to-mouth breathing with a young girl.

Carol turned back toward the door.

"Get the cart!" she yelled. "We've got another girl who isn't breathing!"

As Rita and Carol lifted the young girl from the back seat, Carol took over Rita's job of breathing for Marissa. When the cart arrived, others wheeled Marissa into the emergency room as Carol continued to breathe for her. In the background, she heard the girl's father talking about his wife dying and then heard him praying out loud.

Accompanied by Tessa and Yulanda, the policewoman took Djuan aside as they entered the emergency room.

"Carol, let me be in charge of this case," Carol's partner on duty said. "You've had enough for one night."

Carol returned to the front desk to find Tessa crying and Yulanda looking very frightened.

"They handcuffed my papa," Tessa explained, pointing to a room just off the reception room. Carol followed Tessa to one of the examination rooms, where she found Rita and a backup patrolman trying to calm Djuan.

"At the moment, he's in bad shape," said Rita. "You may want to get a doctor to have a look at him." Djuan was struggling around on the bed as the other officer tried to hold him. His hands were secured to the top of the bed with Rita's handcuffs.

"Can we talk?" Carol asked Djuan. "Your daughter is breathing, and her heart and blood pressure are OK. Can we just talk about it?"

Djuan looked at Carol and quit struggling. "She will die," he shouted. "My wife died and now my Marissa will die. It is not right for her to die . . . but she will. I know she will."

"Take it easy," Carol said. "You're at one of the best hospitals in the state. The emergency room doctor is with her and your own doctor is on the way. We'll take good care of Marissa. You did everything you could."

"My wife. She died too," said Djuan as he tried to roll over and bury his head in the pillow. The handcuffs hurt him as he moved, and soon he was facing Carol again.

"That was my fault," Djuan said. "I stood and watched her die."

Tessa pushed past Rita and sat on the bed next to Djuan.

"Papa," she said, "You would never talk about Mama. Now you must listen to me. I saw. Mama reached for you, and in just a second she was gone because the truck moved. But Papa, you had no time. It all happened too fast."

Djuan stared up at his eldest daughter. Tears came to his eyes, and then he broke down crying. Tessa shielded her father from the view of the others as she leaned over and hugged him. Yulanda joined the two on the hospital bed.

"Sometimes the man cares too much," she explained to Carol and Rita.

Carol motioned Rita out of the room. "I don't think he's crazy," Carol said.

"No, just exhausted and hurting," Rita said.

"Can we get him out of the handcuffs?" Carol asked. As they went back into the room the other nurse appeared.

"She's stable," the nurse told Carol. "She responded to an antiallergic shot, so we're pretty sure that she was having an allergic reaction. Her lungs are clear, but her windpipe was shutting down. The fever and the breathing problem must have been caused by some virus that she is highly allergic to."

Djuan smiled and kissed Tessa and then Yulanda. "I'm OK," he said to Rita. "Unhook me and let me hug my women."

"Tessa," he asked, ". . . are you sure about your Mama?"

"It wasn't your fault, Papa. I remember that moment so well. It seems sometimes like it happened in slow motion, but you had no chance to help."

Djuan breathed a heavy sigh and then lay quietly on the bed as Rita took off the handcuffs.

"Marissa will be fine, and you will find work here," Yulanda said softly.

"You aren't working?" Carol asked Djuan.

"We picked fruit and vegetables this summer," he replied. "But picking is done. Now I will try to find work as a mechanic."

"You're a mechanic?" Carol asked.

"I like it. I worked on cars and machinery while we were in the South."

"Hmmm," said Carol. "I probably shouldn't get your hopes up, but I want you to call my husband at work tomorrow. He just had someone quit at a gas station he owns and needs a new man."

Carol patted Djuan on the shoulder. "Anybody who's loved as much as you are by his wife and kids should be working for my husband."

"We also have business to settle," Rita said, stepping forward, but with a smile. "There's a little matter of speeding and resisting arrest."

Djuan frowned and glared at Rita.

"Not so fast," Rita said. "Don't jump to conclusions."

"The officer saved Marissa's life," Yulanda said, pleading with Djuan not to be angry.

"If you'd stopped," said Rita, "it might have been too late for Marissa. Under the circumstances, I won't be issuing any tickets."

"The family can go in to see Marissa," a doctor said from the doorway.

Yulanda and Tessa led the way, and Djuan picked up Carlo, who had fallen asleep in the waiting room. The family filed into Marissa's room.

As they stood alone in the entry to the emergency room, Carol spoke to Rita.

"It was one hell of a night," she said. "We sure appreciate your help with Marissa and then with Djuan."

"Nights like this make it all worthwhile," Rita replied.

"You bet," said Carol.

SCENE 4
Bob and Carol

"Did you ever wonder whether we'd make it through five years of marriage?" Carol asked Bob. They were having dinner at a fancy restaurant to celebrate their fifth anniversary.

"Not really," said Bob. "I've always thought about us being together."

"Yeah, me too. But don't you ever wonder why our marriage is surviving while so many others aren't?"

"Sometimes. There are probably a hundred reasons. One reason may be that we're both pretty happy and successful."

"That's true now. But we haven't always been successful."

"Well, things haven't been easy, but we've always taken care of our problems—and each other."

"Do you remember when I was going crazy, tied to the house with Evelyn, and I weighed 180 pounds? How long would we have survived if something hadn't changed?"

The waiter brought a bottle of champagne and the conversation stopped. Bob and Carol watched him as he opened the bottle and poured the first glass.

"A toast," said Bob, "to the last five years, and to the next fifty."

"Let's be just as happy as we've been so far," added Carol.

"To us," Bob said, touching Carol's glass with his own.

"To us."

The conversation dwindled as Bob and Carol looked into each others' eyes.

"I'll be back in a moment to take your order," the waiter said.

"Hey! I didn't tell you," Bob finally said. "The station has been making enough money that I'm going to start paying myself a nice salary!"

"Really?" exclaimed Carol. "And what exactly do you mean by 'nice?'"

"Figured it out today, and it looks like I can bring home about $2,000 a month!"

"You're kidding! That's wonderful. Sounds like we'll be rich."

"Yep! I guess so," Bob said with a smile. "You know what's made a big difference? Things really got better after I hired Djuan. He's the hardest-working man I've ever seen. He's been running the station almost by himse1f, and that's allowed me to do a huge amount of repair work. That's where I'm really making the money. . . . And Djuan's even been helping with the repairs. He sure learns fast."

"Is he doing all right otherwise?" Carol asked. "The night I met him he was in pretty bad shape."

"I've got him on full-time," Bob said. "And I gave him a raise. He earns every penny of what I pay him. Also, he asked me to cosign a loan just last week to buy a trailer home. I'd say he's doing pretty well. Yulanda and Tessa are still working for me afternoons and evenings. And I saw Marissa again the other day. She says hello."

"Oh, that's nice," said Carol. "I'm so glad I mentioned to Djuan that you had a job opening. At first I was afraid that he was some kind of a nut."

"Someday I'll be able to afford a second station," Bob said. "I'm going to send Djuan to a couple of industry training programs this year. When the time comes, he'll manage the second station."

"We sure have come a long way. Thinking back, though . . . it really hasn't been easy. There were times when we both felt like throwing in the towel. I'm so glad we didn't give up."

"I know what you mean," Bob said. "And I can't think of anyone I'd rather share all this happiness with."

"Awwh . . ." Carol said, hiding her face to keep him from seeing her blush.

"I have an idea!" said Bob.

"Oh?"

"I've decided I want to go dancing."

Carol was delighted. "Right after dinner?" she asked.

"No, right now."

"We haven't eaten. . . ."

"I know. We'll eat later."

"But what about the champagne?"

"We'll take it dancing with us."

"You've become a bit crazy."

"But of course, my dear," Bob replied, taking Carol's hand and leading her toward the door.

"We'd like reservations for dinner for two in two hours," he told the surprised hostess. "And here's for the champagne," he said, slipping her a twenty-dollar bill.

They drove toward the center of the city.

"Got someplace in mind?" Carol asked.

"You'll see," Bob replied.

He drove into a parking ramp that was all but deserted, and they went around and around the ramp until the spiral led all the way to the top. All around them were the lights of the city, and just to the east was the lake. Across the lake, they could see the lights of distant houses and businesses. Except for Bob and Carol, the top of the parking lot was empty. Bob turned on the car radio, and they got out and began to dance.

"It's wonderful," Carol whispered into Bob's ear.

"What is?" he whispered back.

"The whole thing . . . life . . . even after all the troubles and in spite of its wrinkles and warts . . . it's wonderful."

They stopped moving and held each other as they looked out over the city.

"Right now . . . at this instant . . . I'm happier than I've ever been in my whole life," Bob said softly.

"Do you suppose this is what life is all about?" Carol asked. "Are we on this planet, going through all we do, just so we can be here with each other at moments like this?"

Questions About the Story
MAIN IDEAS AND DETAILS

EXERCISE 1: Main Ideas and Supporting Evidence

Circle the letter of the choice that best completes each sentence. List at least one piece of evidence that supports your answer.

1. Djuan feels that it has been a successful summer because

    a   Yulanda is going to have her baby

    b. he's gotten to travel and meet new people

    c. Tessa and Marissa want to go home and go to school

    d. they have saved money and done a good job

    Evidence:

2. Djuan feels that they should soon start home because

    a. the cigar box is full of money

    b. he'll be laid off soon anyway

    c. Yulanda wants to have her baby at home

    d. he wants to get home before it snows

    Evidence:

3. The doctor who examines Marissa says that

    a. she has asthma

    b. she'll be getting better very soon

    c. she probably has a collapsed lung

    d. he can't tell what is wrong

Evidence:

4. The farm manager

    a. is angry at Djuan for leaving suddenly

    b. hires someone to take their place right away

    c. seems to understand why they leave suddenly

    d. doesn't even know it when they leave

Evidence:

5. During his first week in business at the gas station, Bob

    a. feels that the station is a great success

    b. has to lay off his mechanic

    c. makes $34

    d. doesn't make any profit

Evidence:

6. Bob discovers that Jerry Rafsky has been stealing from him when

    a. he catches Jerry in the station late at night

    b. his inventory shows that supplies are missing

    c. Jerry's friend tells on him

    d. Jerry sells stolen tires to a friend of Bob's

Evidence:

EXERCISE 2: Supporting Evidence for Inferred Ideas

As you know, not all the ideas in a story are directly stated. Some are only implied by events or by the thoughts, words, and actions of the characters.

Each of the following statements is implied in the story. List at least one piece of evidence from the story that supports each statement.

1. Carol is a competent and well-respected nurse.

2. Rita approaches her job with a sense of fairness and a willingness to help other people.

3. Carol feels strongly about helping people, even people whom she doesn't know.

4. Djuan finds out something very important in his conversation with Tessa about his first wife's death.

5. Djuan finally gets a job with a boss who seems to appreciate him.

EXERCISE 3: **Fill in the Blank**

Fill in the blanks with the correct answer from your reading.

1. The farm manager says that he will keep Djuan employed because Djuan is
_____ and _____.

2. During the summer, Djuan and his family save more than
$_____.

3. As he lies in bed in the morning, Djuan detects that something is wrong because _____.

4. Marissa has several symptoms of being sick:
_____, _____, and
_____.

5. The hospital bill comes to $_____. Djuan covers the bill with _____.

6. On the way home, Marissa's condition gets worse. At that point, Djuan figures they are about _____ miles, or
_____ hours, away from home.

7. After seven weeks of work at his new station, Bob makes a profit of
$_____.

8. When Bob decides to keep the station open at night, he hires a young man named _____ who is related to
_____.

9. By the time Djuan passes Rita's squad car he has sped up to almost
_____ miles per hour.

10. At the hospital, Djuan is in such bad condition that Rita has to
_____.

11. On their fifth wedding anniversary, Bob and Carol leave the restaurant before dinner and go _____.

VOCABULARY

EXERCISE 4: Synonyms

> A **synonym** is a word or phrase that means the same or almost the same as another word or phrase.

Below you will find a number of phrases taken from the story. Each phrase contains an underlined word. Think of a synonym for the word and write it in the blank. Then write a sentence using the *original underlined word*. The first one is done for you as an example.

1. The late stages of Yulanda's pregnancy signaled that it was nearly time . . .

   indicated

   Gina signaled to her partner that the coast was clear.

2. . . . when the opportunity arose

   _____

3. . . . separated only by a short partition

   _____

4. Djuan detected one breathing harder.

   _____

5. . . . coaxing her to wake up

   _____

6. Marissa's breathing got increasingly hoarse and raspy.

   _____

7. The doctor appeared to be startled by the question.

   _____

8. The tools that he purchased were clean and new.

   _____

9. At the end of the day Bob <u>tallied</u> his receipts.

_____

10. "I was being <u>straight</u> with you."

_____

11. . . . time to do a careful <u>inventory</u>

_____

12. <u>Momentarily</u> a team of doctors and nurses would be there.

_____

13. "She's <u>stable</u>," the nurse told Carol.

_____

ANSWERS ARE ON PAGES 184–85.

SCENE 5
Paul

Paul used most of his remaining cash to buy a car. He had to move fast because his "job" depended on his having a reliable car, so he settled quickly on an inconspicuous sedan that ran well and had a large trunk.

"It may have been for the best," he thought. "You've got to change your methods of operation, or you're bound to get caught. . . . For all I know they were looking for my old car."

He continued to operate on the fringes of the city, moving around from suburb to suburb. Danger and fear were part of Paul's life, but he was smart enough to realize that some dangers and fears were real, while others were only imagined.

He'd often suspect that he was being followed. As he drove home in the dark, he'd look in the rearview mirror at the headlights behind him and think about what he'd do if the car started to flash red lights.

Paul had discovered that cars often did follow him, but it was simply a matter of the other car going into the city on the same route that he was taking. This happened often enough that Paul decided it didn't pay to even think about it . . . unless he saw the same car more than once.

As Paul woke one morning, he felt trouble, but he didn't yet know why. He hadn't slept well, and his hand shook when he lit his first cigarette. He ate breakfast at Edith and Joe's All Night Diner, around the corner from his room. The food seemed worse than usual, and the waitress seemed openly hostile toward him. He sat for a long time trying to figure out whether things were as bad as they seemed. He wondered why he suddenly felt so worried.

"I'm probably only imagining things," he thought, as he lifted a forkful of cherry pie. "God, it tastes like it's been here since the place opened."

He left the diner and walked back toward his room. It was a sunny and clear morning. The shopkeepers were out on the sidewalks, rolling down their awnings and hosing down the sidewalks in front of their shops. A stream of water ran down the gutter carrying paper and other debris into the storm sewer down the block. Paul began to feel sick.

He lingered for a moment at a flower shop on his block and watched the owner put flowers into a cart on the sidewalk. The flower shop was dark inside, as it was still a good half hour before it would be open for business. The street was quiet except for the sounds made by the shopkeepers as they worked.

But as Paul listened, he heard the distinct sound of a car engine from up the street. He turned in the direction of the sound and saw a man sitting behind the wheel of a black Oldsmobile in the next block. Paul looked away quickly and pretended not to notice, but a feeling of fear swept through his whole body. He'd seen that car before at least once, and perhaps more than once.

"It's probably just my imagination again," he thought. But just to make sure, he walked slowly toward the doorway of the flower shop, thinking that he'd get a second look at the Oldsmobile from behind the flower cart. Once he was behind the flowers, he reached up quickly to make a hole between two bouquets and sneak a look up the street.

A voice behind him said, "Can I help you?"

Paul wheeled around and stared into the darkness of the flower shop. He was unable to see where the voice was coming from, and he felt embarrassed.

"Please don't touch the flowers," the voice said, "unless you're going to pay."

"I was just looking," Paul interrupted, peering harder into the darkened shop.

"You were touching the flowers," said the voice. "Do you want a bouquet? If you touch the flowers, you must pay."

Instead of answering the voice, Paul began walking across the street toward his room. His legs and body felt stiff, and he kept his eyes glued on the door of his building. Once inside, he breathed a sigh of relief, went directly to his room, bolted the door, and sat down. He was certain that the Oldsmobile was a two-door and that it had fender skirts . . . not the kind of car used by the police.

"Wait a minute," he thought. "I only saw the car for a few seconds—not long enough to know those details! I know I've seen that car before. But where?"

There was no use taking a chance on staying in this neighborhood. One room was as good as another. He'd wait until dark, drive his car up to the door, load up his belongings, and then be on his way.

He checked his wallet to see how much cash he had on hand and then remembered the bag behind the grate. He retrieved the bag and rolled the bills around his ankle, fastening them with a rubber band. He slipped on the sock and looked out onto the street from behind the curtain. The car was still there.

"Even if the guy in the Oldsmobile were looking for me, he surely wouldn't wait all day," Paul thought. Tomorrow would be a new day, and he'd be in a new part of town. He started to pack his belongings into a suitcase and some boxes.

The day crept by slowly. Paul passed time drinking beer and watching TV. Later in the afternoon he tried to sleep but was too much on edge. Several times he went to the window to see if the black Oldsmobile was still there. It hadn't moved. At supper time he felt exhausted, and he had to force himself to eat.

"Just make this day pass," he prayed, to nobody.

It was getting late. Paul glanced at his watch and saw that it was close to midnight. He went to the window and relaxed a little; the Oldsmobile had been moved an hour before and had not reappeared.

"Now it's time," he thought. He took his belongings out to the hall and piled them just inside the door that led to the street. When this was done, he opened the door and looked out onto the street. The shops were closed and nobody could be seen. There were cars parked along the street but still no sign of the black Oldsmobile.

Paul entered the street, walking swiftly and staying as close to the shops as possible. To get to his car, he had to go to the end of the block and around the corner. He stopped for a moment in the entry to one of the shops. He realized that he was out of breath, even though he hadn't been running.

He looked back up the street and found that there were still no signs of life. He made his way down the block, and after turning the corner he quickened his pace to the car. He drove back to the front of his building without using his headlights and then stopped. He shifted the car into park and got out, but he left the engine running.

Rounding the car, he opened both doors on the passenger side and then turned to get his belongings from the hallway. The small interior light in the car had come on because one of the front doors was open. Paul would rather have completed his moving in total darkness. He carried a box out and threw it across the back seat. He looked up the street as he headed back to the building.

"So far so good," he thought.

He took a second load out to the car and then realized that he hadn't opened the trunk. He'd have to turn off the car so that he could use the key to open the trunk— but that seemed too risky. Not wanting to be seen on the street, he went back into the hallway to think.

"Why the hell didn't I open the trunk before?" he thought.

Paul looked at his belongings and realized that they would not fit in the back seat. He ran to the front seat of the car, removed the key, and went directly to open the trunk. As he turned the key in the lock, a set of headlights could be seen coming down the street.

"Oh God, he's seen the light from my car," sighed Paul. He stood absolutely still for a moment, watching the approaching headlights. He was torn between getting the rest of his belongings or getting into his car and getting the hell out immediately.

Suddenly he realized that in his state of panic he was standing frozen with his hands on the trunk lid of the car. He had already wasted valuable time.

"I don't even have time to close the doors on the passenger side," he thought, as he grabbed his keys and ran to the front seat. He tried twice to get the key into the ignition and finally succeeded.

"Start," he said, turning the key. "Don't fail me now."

The engine turned over slowly and then came to life.

Paul slammed the shift lever down into drive and punched the accelerator. As the car swerved to the left and raced forward there was the sound of broken glass and metal on metal. Then the interior light of the car went off, and Paul realized that the two open doors on the passenger side had struck a parked car. The force had slammed both doors shut.

He raced up the street toward the oncoming headlights, realizing that he had not turned his own headlights on. The approaching car was in the middle of the street, and Paul thought for a moment that they'd collide head-on. He reached for the light switch and pulled it just in time to make sure he could be seen by the other car. Looking to his left and his right, he wondered if he could drive his car onto the sidewalk.

Upon seeing Paul's headlights, the driver of the approaching car slammed on his brakes. The car veered to the right and came to a stop against the side of a parked car.

Seeing his opening, Paul floored the gas pedal and was approaching fifty miles per hour when he passed the other car. Paul got a glimpse of the driver and other occupants. It looked like a family: the father driving, the mother holding a child, and three or four other children in the back seat.

"I can't go back for my stuff," Paul thought. "Those poor idiots will want to report the accident." He sped through the dark streets listening to the passenger-side doors rattling. He knew they were not shut properly, but he suspected that they were so damaged that they couldn't be shut any better.

"Where do I go now?" he asked himself.

SCENE 6
Ted

Ted was determined to bounce back quickly from what he felt was the end of his relationship with Liz. He would get back into the swing of things by mending old friendships and dating. He later realized that on the very day that Liz was to leave for Florida, he'd had his first date with another woman.

They went to a party at her sorority house. She spent the last hour of the evening convincing Ted that he was too drunk to drive home. Eventually she "poured" Ted into a taxi for the ride home, and Ted left her the keys to his car so that she could deliver it to him the following day.

In the morning, Ted was sick and had trouble sleeping. He suffered through nightmares and awoke several times with the same memory. . . . On Sunday morning he and Liz had been in the habit of jogging long distances together. Then they would go out for breakfast and read the Sunday paper at the restaurant.

On these Sundays, he'd felt healthy and had a feeling of accomplishment about running a long distance. But now, as he lay sick in bed, he felt just the opposite because in addition to being physically sick he felt both guilty and depressed.

At noon his date from the night before called to ask if he was ready for her to bring him the car. Ted explained that he wasn't feeling well, and Jill laughed.

"I suspected that you wouldn't," she said. "That's why I called before I came out." They agreed that Jill would return the car closer to supper time and that they'd go out for supper.

From the beginning, Ted had some doubts about getting involved with Jill. He realized that in many ways she was totally unlike Liz: Liz had always challenged his opinions and statements, but Jill was always agreeable and let him lead. Liz was unconventional, doing what she thought was important regardless of what others thought, but Jill was conventional. In fact, much of Jill's life was structured by the activities of her sorority. Both women were very attractive, but in totally different ways. While Liz was slim and athletic, Jill was soft both in her appearance and her manner.

Ted could not help but make comparisons between the two women, but he soon convinced himself that Jill was more desirable.

"The more different she is the better," he thought to himself. "I don't want such a strong-headed woman as Liz anyway."

Occasionally, but very rarely, Mr. McKenna would mention Liz when he saw Ted at the plant. It was obvious that he was not going to become involved. When he did mention Liz, however, Ted would feel a kind of shudder through his whole body.

On the one hand, he was very curious to know what and how Liz was doing. But on the other hand, he did not want to hear anything about her because for hours or even days after, he would feel again the pain and loss of her leaving.

As time wore on, however, Ted's feelings about Liz faded and almost disappeared against the background of sorority parties, homecoming decorations, and formal dances. Ted had been swiftly drawn into campus high society, and there he found a great deal of comfort in the activities of Jill and her friends.

As Jill entered her senior year at the University, the dating game seemed to become deadly serious. The sorority "sisters" who were also seniors were one by one becoming engaged, and within Ted and Jill's group of friends, the topic of conversation always turned to engagements and marriage.

Jill explained to Ted that the sisters thought their senior year was the best and last chance they'd have to find the right partner. And indeed, that spring, wedding plans spread through their group like an epidemic.

Though he'd never seriously considered what it would mean to be married, Ted found himself in a jewelry store buying an engagement ring for Jill. She accepted the ring, and they joined the proud group of friends who would attend each others' weddings that summer. It was less than a year since Liz had joined the Peace Corps.

Ted had yet to meet Jill's parents. They'd be coming to the University for Jill's graduation, but Ted and Jill decided that it would be best if they talked to her parents about their upcoming marriage before that. Jill made arrangements for her parents, herself, and Ted to spend a spring weekend together at her parents' cottage.

As Ted and Jill approached the cottage, Ted noted how solid it appeared. It was placed high above a lake, growing out of the earth but sheltered by an ancient pine forest. "Solid and secure comfort," he thought.

But then his mind flashed back to a weekend with Liz and her parents in a sailboat far out on the lake. There had been the possibility of storms and trouble, but the trip had left him feeling that he had done something unique and exciting.

That evening Jill's father said, "The world's going to hell in a hand basket. It used to be that if you had a good idea, you could go out and turn a buck. Now you've got environmental committees, federal restrictions on hiring and firing, and a world full of do-gooders to back them all up. Everyone has the idea that businesses are some kind of social welfare agencies and that businessmen should be social workers.

"Let me tell you, what counts in life can be measured by the money you make. All the do-gooders in the world are parasites whom business supports. If I were you, Ted, I'd go into sales, that's where the action is. You keep that money floating by and every time a dollar passes you, you grab yourself a nickel. . . ."

Ted sat for a moment in dazed silence. He remembered Liz's father's sunburned face as they talked together on the boat about his philosophy toward his customers . . . and then his mind flashed to the image of Liz breaking into tears when reading a story about world hunger.

"I know what you mean," said Ted, swallowing hard. But to himself he thought, "Ted, you've entered a world of plastic people."

"You up for a little golf tomorrow?" asked Jill's father.

Again Ted did not respond quickly. All he could think about was that while he sat in solid middle-class comfort, Liz was out in a South American jungle struggling to help people.

"I'd love to play golf," Ted said, trying to sound genuine.

"We've been thinking of buying you and Jill a country club membership as a wedding present. Would you like that?"

Again Ted paused as something deep inside him said to get in his car and leave, but instead he took a sip from his drink and composed himself.

"We'd love to join the country club," he said. "A lot of our friends are joining." But even while he said this, he thought of Liz's warmth and caring and then of a country club bar full of mannequins.

"Can plastic ever feel warm to the touch?" he asked himself. "What the hell am I going to do?"

SCENE 7
Liz

After a year in the Peace Corps, Liz returned home. Earlier she had thought that she'd only be returning for a thirty-day furlough, but her plans changed. After an evening of talking to her parents about her experiences, she told them that she had an idea to share with them.

Housing was a major problem where she had been working. People were crowding into the cities, even though there were no housing units of any kind available. Consequently, major cities were surrounded by areas covered with makeshift shacks. These shacks were constructed out of scrap wood and metal and often had roofs of plastic sheeting. Often there was no running water or toilet facilities.

"I don't see how we can help them make any progress," Liz told her parents, "until the housing and sanitation problems are under control. Housing and sanitation are so basic to everything else that something has to be done there first."

She went on to present to her parents an idea that she'd developed during the year. They got out the family's slide projector, and Liz began to discuss the problem.

"These shots are of how the people had lived for centuries, before they began to crowd into the cities. . . . You can see that several families often shared all or parts of a dwelling. So these people aren't used to a lot of living space or private homes and yards. I want to design an economical dwelling like some of those in the slides, but one that has a kitchen and bathrooms and can be built by people who are not expert carpenters."

Mr. McKenna was sitting forward in his chair, looking with intensity at the slides. Liz could tell that the wheels were turning inside his head.

"Back up a couple of slides," he said. "How often do you see housing like that?"

"That's how many people lived until about fifteen years ago," Liz replied.

"Look at the possibilities," said Mr. McKenna. "Concrete foundations aren't necessary in that climate. You could go with treated lumber, and that would really cut down on the cost. How are the rooms arranged? Where do they do their cooking?"

"Hardly anybody had a private kitchen," Liz explained. "The extended family— aunts, uncles, cousins, and grandparents—all shared cooking facilities."

They talked for several hours about the culture and people and about possible housing. As the night wore on, Liz and her father drew sketches and floor plans of an idea that was quickly taking shape in their minds.

Each unit would house four groups of people. There would be a central kitchen area shared by the four groups of people and four housing wings coming off the kitchen in each direction. The bathroom for each wing would be next to the kitchen. That way even though there were four bathrooms there would be only one central area where plumbing and sewage lines would be installed.

By early morning they had completed the sketches.

"God, this is exactly what they need," Liz said. "The people would accept and appreciate housing like this because it's an updated version of how they've always lived. The problem will be to get it done cheaply and make it simple enough so it can be built by unskilled people who don't have power tools."

"I've got the plan," Mr. McKenna said. "We're going to do the building right here. Every piece will be cut. Doors and windows can be installed right here in the factory, and the bathrooms and kitchens can be shipped as finished units that just have to be put in place and bolted to the four wings.

"The way we've got this sketched out I think we can use sea containers for shipping. Four complete bathrooms could go into one sea container, and the cut pieces for each wing would fit into another container. The kitchen would need its own container. . . . Liz, why don't you work with my architect at the plant, and let's see if you can make this idea fly."

"The other problem is going to be financing. How are these poor people going to afford even really inexpensive housing?"

"Maybe I can help with that. Let's look into the possibility of combined government and private financing. The people wouldn't buy the units, they'd rent them. Some of their rent could go toward a down payment so that they'd eventually own the buildings."

"I'd be working at the plant?" Liz asked.

"Yes," said her father. "I want you in charge of the project. You work with the design department. When you've got an idea fully developed, we'll construct a complete unit and assemble it on that space behind the cutting shed. If we get some pictures of the whole process of assembly and the finished product, you'll have a much easier time selling the idea of financing the project."

"Oh Dad, that's just what I wanted. . . . I have one problem with the whole idea. I don't know how I'm going to handle working with Ted."

"He's still up in accounting. You won't be working with him much, but he has moved up in the company and eventually he'll get involved in the cost analysis."

By Thursday of that week, the company's chief architect had cleared his drawing board and was ready to work with Liz. At first he'd been skeptical, thinking the idea was too farfetched. But by Friday afternoon, Liz could tell that the possibilities had captured his imagination.

Late on Friday, as she left the plant, she saw Ted for the first time in more than a year. As Liz walked out of the entrance to the plant's main building, Ted was just ahead of her.

As he left the building, Liz could see that he was being picked up by a woman driving a new car. The woman got out and walked around the car so that Ted could drive. Liz watched from the shadows of the building as Ted got into the car and kissed the woman. Liz was tempted to stay inside and avoid seeing Ted. "But," she thought, "I might as well get it over with."

As Ted and the woman drove by the entrance, Liz stepped out of the building and waved. Ted looked shocked and stopped the car abruptly. As Liz walked over to the car, he rolled down the window but did not get out.

"H'lo Ted," she said. "Remember me?"

"Hi," he said. His heart was pounding and he suddenly felt weak, but he tried to act calm. "It's been a long time," he said. "Liz, I want you to meet Jill. . . . Jill, this is Liz McKenna."

Liz waved to Jill, who was on the other side of the car. They talked for just a minute, and then Ted said rather suddenly, "We've got to go, Liz. I guess I'll be seeing more of you here at work." But to himself Ted wondered if he could handle working in the same building with Liz.

As the weeks passed, Ted and Liz did not see much of each other because Liz almost never went into the accounting offices. Ted's office, however, had a large window that overlooked a part of the plant where Liz and the architects were to experiment with building and assembling parts of the new housing units.

One morning when Ted got to his office, he looked down to see a truck backing into the plant assembly room. Liz, wearing blue jeans, a hard hat, and work boots, was riding in the back of the truck with a crew of carpenters. She was carrying a roll of blueprints, and when the truck was unloaded she began to put the men to work constructing wall units.

Often that day Ted looked down as the project took shape. Liz was clearly in charge, as the carpenters came to her for advice. But, like her father, she was not one to stand on the sidelines and give orders.

By midmorning Liz had a hammer in her hand and was pounding nails with the crew. By the afternoon, her shirt was soaked with sweat and her hair was falling out of her hard hat. By the time Ted was done for the day, both the outside and inside walls were propped in place, and Liz and the men had begun to put the beams in place for the roof.

As Ted looked down from his window for the last time that day, Liz and the men were sitting inside the newly built structure. She seemed totally at ease with the men as they drank beer, laughed, and talked. Ted lingered for a long time, hoping that nobody would see him staring down at the crew.

"What a woman," he thought. "What a hell of a woman."

SCENE 8
Rita

Having Josh around for five days and then having him leave was as difficult for Sam as it was for Rita. The night after Josh left, Sam wet his bed for the first time in three years. Then he was afraid to sleep alone, and each night he got into bed with Rita. Also, for the first time in months, he had several fights with other children at the day-care center.

"I think I'm being a pain in the neck," he told Rita.

"You can say that again," she replied. "You want to talk about it?"

"When's Josh coming back?" Sam asked.

"I don't know," she said. "I was wondering myself." Now Rita was certain that Sam missed Josh at least as much as she did, and that was a lot.

Rita tried several times to reach Josh at the telephone number that he'd given her, a work number. Each time she was told that Josh was out of town on a teaching assignment. Finally Rita left a message, asking Josh to call her at home, but a week went by and he did not return her call.

Rita had sensed that Josh did not want her to call him at home, but, she thought, the man really left her no choice. She had to know if he was as sincere and caring as he seemed, or if he'd been leading her on.

On a Sunday, she dialed Josh's home number several times, but each time she lost her courage and hung up the receiver before it had a chance to ring. Finally, she allowed the phone to ring, praying to herself that he would be friendly and have an explanation for why he hadn't returned her calls. A woman answered.

Rita sat stunned and unable to speak. Finally, in a state of near panic, she asked for Josh. He wasn't there. She asked the woman to have Josh return her call.

"Could I tell him what it's about?" the woman asked.

"It's OK," Rita blurted. "Just have him call me."

"If this is not a business call, you better know that Josh is taken," the woman said.

"Just have him call," Rita said as she hung up. "Of course he's taken," she thought to herself as she began to cry. "Why wouldn't he be taken?"

On Monday night, Josh finally returned her call. Rita explained what had happened and then asked him directly if the woman was right: "Are you taken?"

"In a manner of speaking, I am," he said. "We live together and have for some time, but I've always seen other women and she knows that."

Rita struggled to keep from sounding angry. "That's not what I want," she said. "You weren't honest with me when you were here."

"I didn't tell you everything," Josh admitted. "How's Sammy?"

"He didn't take it very well. You made a big impression on him and then disappeared. He's having trouble now. . . . It really wasn't fair to him, or to me."

"Sorry," he said.

"Let's leave it at that," Rita said, hanging up the phone.

As time passed, Rita became a sergeant in the police department. Josh returned to the city several times and worked with her in teaching courses at the police academy. When he was in town, he spent time with Rita and Sam.

"I'll be honest with you," she'd told him. ". . . You're just what I want, but we'll only be friends as long as you can't settle down with one woman."

"Not now," he said. "Maybe never."

"That's OK as long as I know where I stand," she replied.

Josh began to phone Rita and Sam, keeping in close contact. He became Rita's close and trusted friend and was like a godfather to Sam. Only on rare occasions did Josh try to get physical with Rita.

"Are you ready to move in with me?" she'd ask when he did.

"Not yet," he'd say.

"Then keep your hands to yourself."

"You like me?" he once asked.

"Only from a distance," she said with a smile.

It was almost by chance that Rita and Liz renewed an old friendship. One day, Liz stopped in at the Candy Hut to see Shirley.

"Oh my God . . . a ghost out of my past," Shirley said as she hugged Liz. "My, you're a beautiful young woman."

"You haven't changed a bit, Shirley. You always had a way of making me feel good. How've you been?"

"Let's talk, girl," said Shirley. "But first I got some old business to settle." Shirley went quickly to the telephone and then returned.

"I got a surprise for you," she said. "Sit down for a while. We're gonna have a talk."

For a while the two women talked about old times. Then Shirley, who was facing the door of the Candy Hut, smiled broadly as someone entered.

"Look behind you," she said.

Liz turned around to find Rita entering the Hut.

"Oh my gosh," she said, getting up.

"I don't believe it. I thought I'd never see you again," said Rita. Then, turning to Shirley she said, "Mama, how did you know?"

"I never told," Shirley said. "Now the cat's gonna come out of the bag. . . . I knew about the Agency for Battered Women because they'd helped you. Later I told Liz it might be a good place to work. Then I come to find out she's working with you. . . . Sit down, Rita."

"Oh, it's wonderful to see you," Rita said to Liz. "I'm trying to remember. When we were doing counseling, did I have anything bad to say about my mama?"

"Not that I can remember," Liz replied. "But I didn't know until this minute that

Shirley is your mother." The three sat for minutes saying nothing, just feeling the strong bonds of friendship that had lasted all that time.

"I got one more surprise for Liz," Shirley said. "I want you to meet the girl workin' behind the counter, but first I got a story to tell. . . ."

"No, Mama," Rita said. "Just have them meet. . . . Don't tell the story."

"I gotta," said Shirley. "I don't ever tell people, but I gotta tell Liz 'cause Liz is like family . . . That girl wouldn't be here if it wasn't for Rita. She was about dead and Rita saved her. Later her daddy wrote a letter to the police department, and Rita got a commendation. Now every once in a while Rita gets flowers delivered at home. . . . The girl's folks send 'em."

Marissa finished doing dishes behind the counter and came over to the booth where the three women were seated.

"Can I get you guys anything?" she asked.

"Just set yourself down here for a minute," Rita said, pointing to the last seat left in the booth.

"Liz, I want you to meet Marissa. She's Mama's right hand woman around here, and whenever I want to boogie, she watches Sam for me." Rita put an arm around Marissa as the four sat and talked.

In a while Marissa got up.

"I've got work to do," she said. "My papa and his boss are coming here for supper after they close the station."

Soon Djuan and Bob entered the shop and sat down at the counter.

"Yulanda and the kids are coming too," Djuan told Marissa. "I hope you have enough food." Then in the mirror Djuan spotted Rita, who was sitting behind him. Djuan turned on the stool and with a giant smile on his face walked across the room and sat next to her. Rita put an arm around Djuan and kissed his cheek.

"He's so shy," she said to Liz and Shirley. "He wants to kiss me back, but he can't bring himself to it."

Djuan smiled and nodded, indicating that Rita was right. Then he shook hands with Liz and Shirley as Rita kissed him again.

"The whole family is coming over," he said. "We're going to celebrate."

"What's the occasion?" Shirley asked.

"You'll see," Djuan said.

"Maybe I better be going," Liz said. "This looks like a private party."

"Not on your life," Rita told her. "None of this would be happening if you hadn't been there that Saturday morning."

Minutes later Carlo entered the Hut, followed by Tessa and Yulanda. Yulanda was slower than the rest because she was leading her youngest child.

Carlo came directly to the booth and climbed into Djuan's lap.

"I want a chocolate sundae," he said. Then he turned to Rita. "Where's Sam?" he asked.

"By God, I'll go and get Sam," Rita said. "Be back in just a minute." She hugged Yulanda as she got up, and Yulanda then sat down at the booth. Djuan grabbed her and kissed her. Yulanda blushed and pushed him away.

"She's really shy," he said with a grin.

As Marissa and Tessa began to prepare the food, Carol and Evelyn entered the Hut. Carol hugged Bob, and together they went over to the booth to join the other adults. Djuan shook Carol's hand and tried to make room for them.

"Thank you for the flowers," Carol said to Djuan, kissing him. "But you really don't have to . . . "

"How's my favorite mechanic?" Shirley asked Bob.

"Doin' good," he replied. "You tell those girls to put some meat in the burgers tonight."

"Don't think I don't know what's been goin' on," Shirley replied. "They always put two patties in your burgers."

When Rita and Sam returned, Bob stood up and asked everyone to be quiet.

"This is a special night for me and Djuan," he said. "So I know it's a special night for all of us. A couple of weeks ago, Djuan finished another part of his training program, and then just today we made a deal on another station. Djuan is going to specialize in doing front-end work at the second station, and Yulanda is going to manage the pumps at both stations."

"What an amazing thing," thought Liz. "All these people who seem so different but who know each other so well." Then Liz noticed that Shirley had started to cry.

"Are you OK?" she asked.

"Oh hell, yes. I'm fine," Shirley said, smiling through her tears. "I'm just a sentimental old fool. . . . I was just sittin' here thinkin' about everyone and about all the work and struggle it took to make this party happen."

Questions About the Story
MAIN IDEAS AND DETAILS

EXERCISE 5: Main Ideas and Supporting Evidence

Provide evidence for the following main ideas by filling in information from the story. Some of these main ideas are stated in the story, but others are only implied.

1. In many respects, Ted's new girlfriend, Jill, is different from Liz. On the left side, list some of Jill's characteristics, and on the right, list some of Liz's characteristics.

Jill	Liz
a.	a.
b.	b.
c.	c.

2. Ted has serious reservations about marrying Jill.

    a.

    b.

3. Liz is like her father in many ways.

    a.

    b.

4. Sam misses Josh when he leaves.

    a.

    b.

5. Shirley is both popular and respected.

    a.

    b.

    c.

6. Djuan is very appreciative of Rita's help on the night Marissa is brought to the hospital.

    a.

    b.

7. As the story ends, Djuan is becoming quite successful.

    a.

    b.

EXERCISE 6: Sequence

Number the following events in the order they occurred in Paul's scene. The first event should be number one.

Paul

____   **a.**   stopped at a flower shop

____   **b.**   got his money out of the grate

____   **c.**   parked his car in front of his apartment

____   **d.**   bought a car

____   **e.**   saw headlights coming down the street

____   **f.**   turned on his headlights

____   **g.**   smashed up the doors on his car

EXERCISE 7: True or False

Indicate whether the following statements are true (*T*) or false (*F*).

____   **1.** Paul manages to get all his belongings into the car.

____   **2.** Ted and Jill go jogging on Sunday mornings.

____   **3.** Ted is happy to be done with Liz.

____   **4.** Ted agrees with Jill's father.

____   **5.** Liz wants to build housing that would be shared by several groups of people.

____   **6.** Liz doesn't get along with the men in her crew.

____   **7.** Liz still has some feelings for Ted.

____   **8.** Because he hasn't been honest, Rita can never be Josh's friend.

____   **9.** Liz has known all along that Rita is Shirley's daughter.

____ **10.** Marissa works at the Candy Hut.

____ **11.** Shirley is Carlo's grandmother.

____ **12.** Djuan specializes in doing front-end work on cars.

____ **13.** Yulanda continues working as a baby-sitter.

READING BETWEEN THE LINES

EXERCISE 8: Understanding the Characters

On a separate sheet of paper, write a short paragraph answer to each of the following questions.

1. As the story ends for Paul, he is very afraid. In fact, his fears are causing him to do things that are not rational or logical. Identify one of his actions that you think is irrational and explain why it is irrational.

2. Explain why Ted might prefer to marry Jill instead of Liz. Give an explanation or reason and then give evidence from the story to support your explanation.

3. Do you think that Ted and Liz will ever get back together? Explain why or why not.

4. Rita and Josh end up becoming good friends in spite of Josh's live-in lover.

    a. Why does Rita refuse to have an affair with Josh?

    b. What does their long-standing friendship seem to be based on?

5. At the party at the Candy Hut, Liz thinks to herself how different all the people there are. Why do you think they care about each other?

EXERCISE 9: Ending the Story

> A **turning point** in someone's life happens when the person makes a critical decision or when an important event occurs. For example, you might think the turning point in Bob's life was when he married Carol. Or you might think Bob's turning point was when he opened his gas station.

You have now completed the *LifeScenes* readings. This final exercise asks you to think back over the readings and identify the event that you feel was the turning point in the life of each of the characters. Then explain why that event was the turning point for that character by telling what its result was. Finally, tell what you think each character will be doing five years after the story's end.

Bob

1. turning point:

result:

2. future of character:

Carol

1. turning point:

result:

2. future of character:

Paul

1. turning point:

result:

2. future of character:

Rita

1. turning point:

    result:

2. future of character:

Liz

1. turning point:

    result:

2. future of character:

Ted

1. turning point:

    result:

2. future of character:

Djuan

1. turning point:

    result:

2. future of character:

ANSWERS ARE ON PAGES 185-86.

Answer Key

Chapter 1

EXERCISE 1—pages 5-6

Your answers may not be exactly the same as the ones given here. Did you give at least one piece of evidence that relates specifically to the main idea in the question?

2. b His father says he was a stud and a boozer when he was young, but he's always on Bob's case about those same things *(page 2)*.

3. d He has been staring defiantly at her all year *(page 2)*.

4. a There are eight or ten tape decks in the room *(page 3)*. He could steal a stereo out of a locked car in three minutes *(page 3)*. His "work" makes it important that he and Annie not look well off or be noticed by their neighbors *(page 5)*.

5. c "If you become part of the system, you can kiss your freedom good-bye" *(page 4)*. When people moved west they didn't have rules or police. They had freedom, and when they didn't like what happened, they could move on *(page 4)*.

6. b It is important not to look too well off *(page 5)*.

EXERCISE 2—page 7

1.	h	**6.**	e
2.	a	**7.**	c
3.	i	**8.**	d
4.	f	**9.**	b
5.	g	**10.**	j

EXERCISE 3—page 7

You may not have answered in exactly the same way as these answers. Did you answer the questions in your own words?

1. a. One compartment likes to talk about how wild he was as a teenager.

b. The other compartment wants to discipline his son.

2. a. Paul lives in a one-room apartment.

b. The only thing he really has to have to survive is $500.

c. His parents told him never to ask them for help from then on.

EXERCISE 4—pages 7-8

Here are some possible responses to these questions. You may not have the same answers, and you may not agree with these answers.

1. She would probably describe him as annoying and rude. She might say he doesn't have a proper appreciation for literature or for learning in general.

2. If Bob dropped out, Bob would be agreeing with Paul's point of view. Bob's dropping out would help Paul justify his own decision to drop out.

3. Paul thinks people should live outside the system. He might think this way because the system never gave him anything—for example, his parents don't seem to care about him, and he didn't like school.

EXERCISE 5—pages 12-13

You may have chosen different evidence than that listed in the answers below. Check your evidence to be sure it supports the correct answer.

1. a Though she says very little, kids know that Shirley listens and understands (page 8). She has a reputation for being tough but fair (page 8).

2. c She is able to move freely between the different groups of students in and around school (page 9).

3. b There is some mystery about why Liz chooses to spend time at the Hut (page 9).

4. c The thought of being alone in the apartment is appealing (page 10).

5. c The problem is she has no idea whether it is really leading anyplace different at all (page 10). Maybe the best she could hope for would be to live just like her parents (page 10).

6. d Laughing at him would make him a part of the group. Ted's real fear is that they would ignore anything he said (page 11).

EXERCISE 6—page 13

1.	F	6.	F
2.	T	7.	F
3.	T	8.	F
4.	F	9.	T
5.	F	10.	F

EXERCISE 7—pages 13-14

You may not have answered just like this. Be sure you answered each question in your own words in complete sentences.

1. a. The jocks run the school. They are popular and think they're big shots.

   b. The Hutters don't really feel at home in school, and they're more

comfortable at the Candy Hut. They don't step on other people.

2. She fears her life will be just like her parents', and she is afraid she isn't going anywhere. It would be worse to be unhappy alone than with a partner.

3. When he sits down, they look at the clock or down at their notebooks without saying anything. He doesn't want them to see the fruit pie because they call people they don't like "fruitcakes."

EXERCISE 9—pages 19-20

You may have chosen different evidence than that listed in the answers below. Check your evidence to make sure it supports the correct answer.

1. c She had quit high school without considering the importance of the decision. The future had seemed distant and beyond concern. They had lived for the moment (page 15).

2. b "I'll pretend to be asleep" (page 16).

3. a "Got any food? I'm hungry as a bear" (page 16). He has the funny grin on his face that appears only when he has had a lot to drink (page 16).

4. c Recently the family had moved into a trailer owned by Djuan's cousin (page 18).

5. b Carlo is the baby of the family (page 18). Marissa is still a child (page 18). Tessa is two years older than Marissa (page 18). No other children are mentioned.

EXERCISE 10—pages 20-21

Rita		Djuan	
a.	3	a.	4
b.	8	b.	3
c.	4	c.	2
d.	5	d.	1
e.	1	e.	5
f.	2		
g.	6		
h.	7		

EXERCISE 11—page 21

1.	g	7.	j
2.	e	8.	a
3.	b	9.	d
4.	f	10.	c
5.	i	11.	h
6.	k		

EXERCISE 12—pages 21-22

Here are some sample sentences containing synonyms. You may have chosen different synonyms. If you're not sure your synonym is right, check it and the original underlined word in the dictionary.

2. My boss is <u>requiring</u> that I work twelve-hour days in order to finish this project.
3. I <u>detect</u> a note of sarcasm in your story about my wife.
4. A <u>certain</u> kind of chocolate pie is the only food that kid will eat.
5. When his date rang the doorbell, he <u>leaped</u> to answer it.
6. A man on the train was <u>staring</u> at me all the way home.
7. My cat <u>looks like</u> a tiny tiger.
8. Jonathan is <u>contented</u> as long as he can eat, sleep, and sing.

EXERCISE 13—pages 22-23

You may have different answers than the ones given below. You may not even agree with these answers. If you're unsure about any of your answers, check back in the reading. Do you have evidence for your answer?

1. **a.** Sam: curious, very young child, intelligent
   b. William: drinks heavily, unpredictable, dangerous
   c. Djuan: religious, loves his family, cares about his home
   d. Marissa: obedient, looks like a boy, between Tessa and Carlo in age
   e. Rita: feeling troubled about her marriage, afraid of her husband, unsure of herself
2. Djuan feels sympathetic toward the man. He knows he could be the one who has no job and no money. He feels lucky to have what he has.
3. happy
   a. He smiles as he looks around the dinner table.
   b. His family has a real home they can take pride in.
   c. He feels lucky to have work and a family and to be in America.
4. Rita has trouble concentrating because she is uncertain and troubled. Also, her mind seems to need to escape from thoughts that could be painful.
5. He is relieved when Rita tells him they

are going to Shirley's house. He closes his eyes and falls asleep in Shirley's arms.

Chapter 2

EXERCISE 1—pages 29-30

2. F
3. T The thought of being thrown out scares him.
4. T She wonders whether you just get swept through doors because you don't have another plan.
5. T Her boss schedules her full-time and gives her a raise.
6. F

EXERCISE 2—page 30

1. e   4. c
2. d   5. b
3. a

EXERCISE 3—page 30

1. T   6. F
2. F   7. T
3. T   8. T
4. T   9. F
5. T   10. T

EXERCISE 4—pages 30-31

You probably didn't answer these questions in the same way as the answers given below. Be sure you wrote your answers in your own words and in complete sentences.

1. Bob's father says Bob is all he has in the world, and he tells him to stay out of trouble.
2. Her boss just keeps giving her full-time hours without ever asking her if she wants them.
3. **a.** Janet is an emergency room nurse, and she saves someone's life.
   b. At first Carol feels complimented. Then she doubts that she is really like Janet since Carol is content to be a grocery store cashier.

EXERCISE 7—pages 37-39

You may not have chosen the same evidence as that given in the answers below. Check to be sure your evidence supports the correct answer.

1. b She thinks she will return ready to

become a successful student at the University *(page 32)*.

2. c She is embarrassed because she is still wearing her underwear *(page 33)*.

3. d She tells John she would like to know more about herself *(page 33)*.

4. b She begins to feel a sense of control over her body and mind. With the sense of control comes a sense of responsibility *(page 34)*.

5. d She can't believe he can make it on his own *(page 35)*. He wants his own apartment with a pool, no less *(page 35)*. She wonders how long his success will last *(page 35)*. She lived at home for three years before she got married. She and Ted's father were saving for a place of their own *(page 35)*.

6. d After he finishes work and punches out, he hangs around the computer room asking people questions about their work and how the computer operates. Eventually they get Ted involved in doing some of the work *(pages 36–37)*.

EXERCISE 8—page 39

Here are some sample sentences with antonyms. If you're not sure of your antonym, check it and the original underlined word in a dictionary. Do they have opposite meanings?

2. My failed attempt at pulling the tablecloth out from under the dishes made quite a mess.

3. Urban plazas of steel and concrete replace natural scenery for thousands of downtown dwellers.

4. Linda carefully put one foot in front of the other on the straight white line.

5. Martin had a leisurely breakfast with his seven brothers and four sisters at the family reunion.

6. The forward motion of the car reassured the escaping convicts.

7. The mellow twilight softened every line on his craggy face.

8. We pledged to spend our lives together.

9. Her outdated, glittering shoes caught my eye as she staggered down the platform.

10. Bruce's sturdy legs can carry him for miles on the trail.

EXERCISE 9—pages 39-40

You probably didn't answer these questions in quite the same way as the answers given below. To check your answers, make sure you have evidence from the story. Did you write in complete sentences?

1. a. the six-mile run and nude swimming
It turns part of her world upside down when she realizes she is embarrassed because she isn't nude. It makes her realize that she has a lot to learn about herself and that she might be questioning herself and her life a lot during this camp.

b. her solo
She begins to feel that her life has a purpose and that she has to take responsibility for it. She also realizes that she is in control of herself and her life.

2. She decides to be a part-time student and work part-time. She doesn't think being just a student would have real meaning and purpose. She doesn't want to wait four years to do something important with her life.

3. He learns a lot about the computers on his own time during the evenings. He shows a genuine interest in how they run. Then he does a good job and learns very quickly when he first starts working in the computer room on the day shift.

EXERCISE 10—page 40

You probably didn't answer these questions in quite the same way as the answers given below. To check your answers, make sure you have evidence from the story. Did you write in complete sentences? Did you show similarities when the question asked you to compare? Did you show differences when the questions asked you to contrast?

1. John wants to spend a long time alone with Liz and find out a lot about their relationship. Liz wants to find out more about herself and be on her own.

2. They both want to prove their independence.

3. Ted can afford his own apartment in a place with a pool and tennis courts, and he is just out of high school. His mother had to save for three years so she and Ted's father could live in a place of their own when they married. Their place was only three rooms in the back of her aunt's house.

EXERCISE 11—page 46

1. **a.** Rita will have to live on her baby-sitting money
   b. she is afraid of what William might do to her if she tries to put aside any money
2. she put the dozen roses in the disposal
3. the foreman says he's one of the best workers
4. $100 \times \$.57 = \$57$
5. **a.** the company has been sold
   b. the new owners will make more money by shutting down the foundry
6. **a.** he is older
   b. he was born outside the United States
   c. he didn't go to high school

EXERCISE 12—page 47

1.	d	7.	h
2.	g	8.	j
3.	i	9.	a
4.	e	10.	f
5.	b	11.	c
6.	k		

EXERCISE 13—page 47

You probably didn't answer these questions in the same way as the answers given below. Did you write in your own words? Did you write in complete sentences?

1. He wants to make up to her for beating her.
2. He doesn't like it at all. For example, when she wanted to get a job outside their home, he got very upset and angry, and he disappeared for more than a day.
3. Rita is supposed to call Shirley at the Candy Hut. Shirley will call the police and tell them to go stop Rita and William's fight. Then Shirley will come over to make sure Rita is safe and take Rita home with her if necessary.
4. Rita wants to ask Shirley to baby-sit Sam while Rita and William go out to dinner.
5. He cannot come inside her apartment, lay a hand on her, or threaten her in any way.
6. He works in a foundry, where he grinds rough edges off metal plates that will be made into street signs.
7. The foreman says part of Djuan's pay has

been going to the government as long as he has been working, and now Djuan will be getting part of it back.

Chapter 3

EXERCISE 1—pages 53-54

1.	c	5.	d
2.	d	6.	a
3.	b	7.	c
4.	a		

EXERCISE 2—page 54

a.	2	**e.**	1
b.	6	**f.**	3
c.	4	**g.**	5
d.	7		

EXERCISE 3—pages 54-55

Here are some sample sentences using the matched words. If you're not sure of the meaning in your sentence, look up the word in a dictionary.

2. g Manuel's <u>forwardness</u> shocks his older sisters.
3. d She <u>came to like</u> spending hours on the phone late at night with her mysterious caller.
4. i A genie popped out of a bottle and granted Lydia her <u>wish.</u>
5. b No matter how often Tom gives me that absurd excuse, I will not let him <u>bother</u> me.
6. e The <u>broad</u> avenue was lined on both sides by thousands of chanting protesters.
7. h We have to keep the calico cat and the gingham dog <u>apart</u> from each other.
8. c I don't understand how anyone could think Arnold is <u>gorgeous.</u>
9. a You may have <u>fantasized</u> about going out with me, but that's all you're going to do.

EXERCISE 6—page 60

You probably didn't answer in exactly the same way as the answers given below. Did you summarize by giving only the essential information?

1. **Story 2:** He brought the Vice President of the United States to the plant without warning anyone. He asked workers to tell the Vice President what they did.

Story 3: He found out on a Friday afternoon that a job in another city was running behind. Instead of waiting until Monday, he took the best carpenters and electricians to the site to work over the weekend. He offered them a big bonus if they caught up.

2. Mr. McKenna works hard. He is comfortable with all kinds of people. He cares about his business and the people who work for him.

3. A lot of little things about Paul and his habits have made the landlord suspicious, and he wants to protect his reputation and the other tenants' safety.

4. He could not enter legally without a search warrant.

5. The landlord does not want to be known as someone who rents to criminals. He also does not want other tenants to be disturbed by Paul's noise or be put in danger because of Paul's activities.

EXERCISE 7—page 61

You probably didn't answer these questions in quite the same way as the answers given below. Did you answer in your own words in complete sentences?

1. Mr. McKenna's company keeps finding ways to do things better.

2. Ted is flattered that Mr. McKenna would think Ted was worth educating. But he also thinks that maybe he hasn't pushed himself enough.

3. The landlord takes the tools so that he can pretend to be making repairs if he is caught in the apartment.

4. He finds a lot of stereos and tape players.

5. They are going to watch him until he turns eighteen and then arrest him.

EXERCISE 8—pages 61-62

1. Here are three qualities. You may have thought of others.
   a. loyal
   b. hard working, dedicated to the job
   c. on the lookout for ways the company could improve

2. Ted is shocked because she is his boss's daughter.

3. a. He takes his tools with him so he could pretend to be working on the heating system.
   b. He acts very surprised when the policeman won't come into the apartment.

EXERCISE 9—page 62

Your answers may not be exactly the same as the ones below.

1. a. Paul would believe that the landlord does not have the right to search the apartment. He would say that he pays rent for the room and he should be free to do as he pleases.
   b. The landlord would want to search the apartment. He would say that he has the right to protect his property.
   c. You might have thought that the other tenants would feel one of the following ways:

   They may be glad that the landlord searches Paul's apartment because they may not want to live in the same building as a thief.

   They may not want the landlord to have the right to search Paul's apartment because they may not want their own apartments searched.

2. a. From Paul's point of view, the police should not search the apartment. They have no search warrant and no evidence against him.
   b. From the landlord's point of view, the police should search the apartment. It's obvious to him that Paul has been involved in illegal activities, so they should go in and arrest him.
   c. The other tenants might again have mixed feelings. They might want the police to get Paul. But they also might not like the idea that if Paul's apartment can be searched, their own apartments can be too.

3. Answers will vary.

EXERCISE 10—page 67

You may not have chosen the same evidence as that given below. Does your evidence support the main idea?

1. It troubles Rita to think that Sam might be trying to grow up to be like his father (*page 63*).

2. William threatens to sue Rita for custody. She can't afford to hire a lawyer for a custody battle, and she worries that a public defender wouldn't do a good job. (*page 63*).

3. Sometimes Rita feels sad, lonely, and afraid (*page 63*). She feels she will explode if she doesn't have someone to talk to (*page 63*). She goes back to the Agency for Battered Women for help (*pages 63–64*).

4. She decides to go to the community college for vocational counseling, and she says she feels better after talking to Liz. Also, she wants to go back to talk to Liz again *(page 64)*.

5. Tessa quits school to make money by baby-sitting *(page 65)*. When Djuan makes her go back to school, she gets a paper route. Marissa helps with the paper route *(page 66)*.

6. Djuan reads the help-wanted ads every day and applies for many jobs *(page 65)*.

7. Djuan makes Tessa quit the baby-sitting job so she can go back to school *(page 66)*.

EXERCISE 11—pages 67-68

1.	T	7.	F
2.	F	8.	T
3.	F	9.	F
4.	T	10.	F
5.	F	11.	T
6.	T	12.	F

EXERCISE 12—pages 68-69

If you're not sure you used the word correctly in your sentence, look it up in a dictionary and be sure you understand its meaning.

2. c Forbid that man to ever enter this house!

3. b My cooking is adequate, but I'm no gourmet.

4. a The little boy dreaded his first day of school.

5. a The prisoner is in custody at Cook County Jail.

6. b I hear that the vocational school has a good program in data processing.

7. c My family's custom is to hold hands together in silent prayer before dinner.

8. a If I go back to school, Ephraim's mother will try to interfere.

EXERCISE 13—pages 69-70

You may not have answered these questions in the same way as the answers given below. You may not even agree with these answers. Do you have evidence from the story for your answers?

1. **a.** Bob won't come to Carol's apartment for dinner.

   b. He goes back to her apartment on the night she kisses him.

2. **a.** Paul continues to steal car stereos.

   b. The police are going to arrest him on his eighteenth birthday.

3. **a.** Rita needs someone to talk to, and she doesn't want to upset her mother.

   b. Yes. She finds someone to talk to and starts to see things she can do to get her life moving.

4. **a.** Tessa quits school and gets a job baby-sitting.

   b. Yulanda goes to work outside their home.

   c. Djuan seems to change his belief about Yulanda's role. He accepts her working.

   d. He does not change his belief about Tessa and Marissa's role. He insists that they go back to school.

Chapter 4

EXERCISE 1—page 78

1. she would barely be able to afford to live on half-time pay, much less put money aside for getting married

2. Bob asks Carol to move in with him

3. Carol's mother finds Bob and Carol together in Carol's apartment in their bathrobes on a Saturday morning

4. he would have the privileges of an adult, but he could get into real trouble with the law

5. arrest him

EXERCISE 2—pages 78-79

1.	i	7.	b
2.	f	8.	d
3.	k	9.	g
4.	e	10.	h
5.	j	11.	a
6.	c		

EXERCISE 3—pages 79-80

Here are some possible synonyms and antonyms and some sample sentences. If you're unsure of your synonyms and antonyms or your sentences, look up the words in a dictionary. Do your synonyms mean the same or almost the same as the original word? Do your antonyms mean the opposite?

2. **synonym:** suddenly

   antonym: slowly

   After I told him the bad news, he turned abruptly away, but not before I saw tears glistening in his eyes.

   The gorilla consumed the huge banana very slowly.

3. **synonym:** difficult
   antonym: easy
   I had a <u>grueling</u> experience with David at the emergency room after he was hit by a Hostess Twinkie truck.
   This word processing program is very <u>easy</u> to learn.
4. **synonym:** nervous
   antonym: at ease
   Susan is very <u>anxious</u> because she is afraid Max will quit his job.
   You will certainly feel <u>at ease</u> in this department because the people are wonderful.
5. **synonym:** blocking
   antonym: allowing
   This new file cabinet is <u>obstructing</u> my view of enemy territory across the hall.
   Now that he is married, Mannie has stopped <u>allowing</u> his dog to sleep in his bed.
6. **synonym:** separated
   antonym: close to
   I feel terribly <u>isolated</u> from the human race when I work alone at the office late at night.
   Kathie is very <u>close to</u> her mother and sisters, but she never sees her brothers at all.
7. **synonym:** compliance
   antonym: defiance
   Blind <u>obedience</u> is OK in a dog, but I don't think it's a healthy trait in a person.
   In <u>defiance</u> of company policy, my supervisor hired her own sister to work in the plant.

EXERCISE 5—page 85

You will probably have answered these questions a little differently than the answers given below. Did you include accurate, important details? Did you write in complete sentences?

1. **a.** In his accounting class, Ted objects to having to do accounting by hand when it could be done on a computer. Sometimes he does his assignments on the company computer and copies the answers onto ledger sheets.
   b. In his sociology class, he is a leader in arguing against the professor's position that people need a strong government to regulate their lives.
2. Ted sees Liz jogging, and he can't take his eyes off her. He turns around to look at her as his car passes her, and he hits a tree.
3. Ted hears steel bend and glass shatter; then he loses consciousness. He is thrown into the passenger seat. The radiator bursts and covers the car with steam.
4. **a.** Liz decides not to move Ted's head. She decides not to try to make a bandage.
   b. She applies pressure to his cut to stop the bleeding. She checks his breathing twice.
5. Ted says "I must be dreaming," and "Or else I'm in heaven."

EXERCISE 6—pages 85-86
a. 6   **e.** 5
b. 4   **f.** 1
c. 3   **g.** 2
d. 7   **h.** 8

EXERCISE 8—pages 90-91
1. d   **4.** b
2. c   **5.** a
3. c

EXERCISE 9—pages 91-92
1. counselor
2. three out of five
3. to work with people and to work outdoors
4. cop
5. eight
6. make a living, be a mother, and be a student
7. Big Wheel
8. young
9. a relationship with a man
10. closing, unemployment, applicants
11. unemployment compensation
12. picking fruits and vegetables
13. at the end of the summer
14. smoke coming from the exhaust pipe
15. a leg cramp

EXERCISE 10—pages 92-94
You may not have answered these questions in the same way. In fact, you may not even agree with these answers. Do you have evidence for your answers?
2. **a.** loneliness and embarrassment
   b. She isn't used to going out alone, and she thinks other people will laugh at her because she's by herself.

3. **a.** loneliness and sadness
   b. She's used to having her life revolve around William. His being gone leaves an emptiness that wants to be filled.
4. **a.** joy
   b. He's a little kid playing with his favorite toy.
5. **a.** frustration and guilt
   b. He can't make anyone understand what a good worker he is, and he can't provide for his family.
6. **a.** fear and alarm
   b. She has bad memories of her mother dying when the family was picking sometime in the past.
7. **a.** sadness and fear
   b. She's leaving her home, and the future must seem very uncertain to her. Picking is hard work, and the summer will be hard on her because of her pregnancy.
8. **a.** alarm and worry
   b. The family is totally dependent on the car now that they have left home, and they don't have money for repairs.

Chapter 5

EXERCISE 1—pages 101-102
You may have chosen different pieces of evidence than those listed in the answers below. Does your evidence support the correct answer?

2. d   She hears them fighting, then she tries to hold back tears (page 96).
3. c   At first Bob is impressed with his father's energy, but by ten-thirty he can see that the old man is running out of gas (page 96).
4. a   They return to find that Bob's boss has bought a second gas station. He asks if Bob is willing to manage it (page 97).
5. d   Carol unexpectedly bumps into him, and he tells her he has cancer and it's getting the best of him (page 97).
6. d   He hides for two days in a friend's garage, and not even his friend knows he is there (page 100).
7. b   She can't join Paul unless she changes her identity, and she isn't willing to (page 100).
8. b   She says, "It's really too late," and "I'm with Jamie now, and that's the way it has to be" (page 100).

EXERCISE 2—pages 102-103
1. August
2. large and muscular
3. Joe and Hilda
4. Joe
5. Carol's father
6. the old man's face
7. have the baby
8. a friend's garage
9. Chicago
10. the suburbs around Chicago

EXERCISE 3—page 103
1. F
2. F
3. T
4. F
5. T
6. F
7. T
8. F

EXERCISE 4—pages 103-104
1. He keeps the conversation light at dinner, talking about old times to avoid bringing up his cancer (page 97). He would claim he never felt better (page 99).
2. His energy turns to bitterness and anger, and he rages against being confined in the hospital. Bob and Carol seem to do everything wrong (page 99).
3. He promises that if he lives to see a granddaughter, he will give her a $1,000 savings bond (page 99).
4. When his health slips fast toward the end, he becomes quiet and depressed (page 99).
5. He lives another six days appearing healthy and at peace, and he seems reconciled to the fact of his coming death (page 99).

EXERCISE 6—page 111
1. building a house for his family, realizing it was worth twice as much as he put into it, and deciding to build more houses and sell them
2. You may have chosen two of the following, or you may have thought of others.
   his credit rating
   his reputation
   keeping his customers satisfied
   hard work
3. **a.** doing as well as they can at whatever they're doing
   b. taking pride in their work
4. You may have chosen two of the following, or you may have thought of others.

straightforwardness
physical strength
wealth
success
good looks
intelligence

EXERCISE 7—pages 111-12

1. he thinks the person could be Liz
2. she didn't have to ask where his room was, so he didn't hear her coming
3. she can see the good effect of something she has done
4. they are rich, he doesn't know whether Liz thinks of him as a friend or a boyfriend, and he wonders if she feels sorry for him because of the accident
5. she seems genuinely interested in him and she doesn't seem to judge or evaluate what he says
6. he never missed a payment on a bill, he kept out of debt, and he banked at the same bank for a long time

EXERCISE 9—pages 117-18

You may not have answered in the same way as the answers below. If your answers are different, look back to the questions and the reading to be sure you have really answered the question.

1. a. She looks for the mailman several times a day.
   b. "I'm counting on it so much. . . . I won't be able to take it if I'm rejected."
   c. She is afraid to read the letter because of what might be in it.
2. Rita is continuing to see Liz. She calls Liz to tell her the news as soon as she gets the acceptance letter.
3. a. It is an academic challenge. She has to study law, psychology, arrest procedures, and English.
   b. It is a physical challenge. There are classes in conditioning, subduing a criminal, using weapons, and driving in pursuit of a criminal.
   c. Women are treated identically to men and expected to perform as well as men.
4. a. Sam begs her to go into his day-care center with him the first day she wears her uniform.
   b. Shirley says Sam has told her how proud he is.

5. a. The furniture consists of only cots and a table and chairs. There are no real walls.
   b. They have a hot plate, running water, and electricity but no refrigerator.
   c. The bathrooms are in a separate building.
6. a. Tessa says she had forgotten what hard work picking is, and she might fall asleep while she's eating.
   b. Yulanda is almost too tired to eat.
   c. Yulanda's back and legs are stiff.
7. a. The manager says Djuan has a knack for mechanics.
   b. The manager would never have guessed that Djuan had never worked on engines before.

EXERCISE 10—page 118

Rita		Djuan	
a.	3	a.	2
b.	5	b.	4
c.	1	c.	8
d.	6	d.	5
e.	2	e.	7
f.	4	f.	1
		g.	6
		h.	3

EXERCISE 11—pages 119-20

You may have chosen different synonyms than the ones listed below. If you're not sure of your synonyms or your sentences, look up the words in a dictionary.

2. anticipation
   I lived through a week of agony and <u>suspense</u> until Laura called to say she was safe.
3. turned down
   Jim was <u>rejected</u> by his best friend, but his other friends are standing by him.
4. getting
   Margaret is <u>retrieving</u> the book from the library slot with a bent coat hanger.
5. with embarrassment
   Bonita <u>sheepishly</u> admitted that she had washed the white dress with the purple towels.
6. completely
   I am <u>absolutely</u> convinced that there is no way to finish this project by tomorrow.
7. the same as

Clarence and his brother Garrison talk <u>identically</u>.

8. event

My wedding day was a blissful <u>occasion</u>.

9. temporary

Selling beer and hot dogs at the ballpark is <u>seasonal</u> work.

10. dirty

That <u>soiled</u> diaper smells disgusting.

11. quick

You'll regret your <u>hasty</u> decision to move to Mudpuddle with that man.

12. twilight

The blue-gray light at <u>dusk</u> was the perfect romantic setting for the party, but a mosquito ruined my first kiss.

Chapter 6

EXERCISE 1—pages 126-28

1. d She misses the excitement and contact with other adults. She regrets not using her nurse's training *(page 122)*.

2. d Evelyn requires much more attention than he had thought. Every time he starts a task, she begins to cry *(page 124)*.

3. c The hospital pays as much for half-time as the clinic does for full-time *(page 124)*. Her schedule would be two days a week and every other weekend. Evelyn could be watched by Carol's mother during the week and by Bob on the weekend *(page 124)*.

4. c Within three months, she has lost the extra weight and her depression is gone. Bob realizes that what is better for Carol and Evelyn is better for him too *(pages 124–25)*.

5. a The bank could pass on information about him to the police or to the Internal Revenue Service *(page 125)*.

6. c The government keeps track of purchases like real estate and cars to be sure people pay their taxes *(page 125)*.

7. b He can't find his car when he comes out of the movie. Then he notices the sign at the curb that says "No Parking 4–6 P.M." He realizes that it's past 4:30 *(pages 125–26)*.

EXERCISE 2—page 128

1. F	5. F
2. T	6. T
3. T	7. F
4. F	8. T

EXERCISE 3—pages 128-29

You may have chosen different synonyms and antonyms than the ones listed below. If you're not sure of your answers, look up the words in a dictionary.

	Synonym	**Antonym**
1.	cherish	detest
2.	demanding	relaxed
3.	ironically	sweetly
4.	misery	happiness
5.	simple	elaborate
6.	evil	loving

EXERCISE 5—pages 132-33

You may have chosen other details than the ones listed below. If so, check back in the reading to make sure that you have answered each question accurately.

1. a. jogging together
   b. a three-day bicycle trip
   c. cheering for her at her first marathon
   d. Christmas with her and her parents
2. a. beautiful
   b. intelligent
   c. full of life
3. a. "It's something that I have to get out of my system."
   b. "You're pushing me into a corner."
   c. "You'll do fine without me."

EXERCISE 6—page 133

1. She puts her resumé on file, interviews for several jobs on campus, and is flown to Minneapolis and Houston for second interviews.
2. She wants to help people.
3. The people she would work for really need help, and it's terribly important to her to do something like this.

EXERCISE 9—pages 139-40

You may have chosen different evidence to support the statements. Check to make sure your evidence is accurate and that it supports the statement.

1. Rita says, "It's time" *(page 136)*.
2. Rita worries that he will think she is too forward *(page 135)*. Rita tells Josh not to

call her baby and to call her Officer Ahlgetti in class *(page 135)*.

3. Josh and Sam talk to each other in an easy way when Sam is in the tree *(page 136)*. Josh picks him up, and Sam allows himself to be held, the morning after William's visit *(page 137)*.
4. Rita stops William's slap in midair and considers using her police training on him *(page 137)*.
5. Deep down, Djuan wonders if the manager will honor his promise to fix Djuan's car *(page 137)*.
6. His first wife's face pleads in his memory *(page 138)*. He has asked himself a thousand times why he didn't help her *(page 138)*.
7. Yulanda beams, Tessa and Marissa shout, and Djuan says, "I just couldn't believe that I'd done something that hard" *(pages 138–39)*.

EXERCISE 10—page 140

Rita		Djuan	
a.	4	**a.**	6
b.	1	**b.**	4
c.	3	**c.**	3
d.	2	**d.**	7
e.	5	**e.**	1
f.	6	**f.**	5
		g.	2

Chapter 7

EXERCISE 1—pages 153-54

You may not have chosen the same evidence as that listed in the answers below. Check to make sure your evidence supports the answer.

1. d The farm manager lays off all the workers except Djuan and his family. The farm manager tells Djuan he's a good worker. The cigar box contains over $3,600 *(page 142)*.
2. c He remembers his promise to take Yulanda home before the baby is born *(page 143)*.
3. d He says, "There's just no way to tell what's wrong" *(page 143)*.
4. c Instead of getting upset, the farm manager tells them to come back anytime they need work *(page 144)*.
5. d By the end of the week, Bob realizes that he has spent almost fifty hours at the station and has nothing to show for his time and energy *(page 145)*.
6. b When Bob takes inventory, he becomes certain that he has lost $2,000 in supplies. His accountant says that someone is stealing from him, and Bob immediately suspects Jerry *(page 147)*.

EXERCISE 2—pages 154-55

You may not have chosen the same pieces of evidence. Make sure that your evidence really supports the statement given.

1. When the first dying girl comes in, Carol moves fast to help, and the orderly obeys her orders *(page 148)*. Later, the doctor asks her to be the one to tell the parents that their daughter couldn't be saved *(page 149)*.
2. As soon as Rita catches Djuan in the emergency room driveway, she begins caring for Marissa *(page 149)*. Later, she handcuffs him, but she is concerned about him and tells Carol that he may need a doctor *(pages 149–50)*. Then she doesn't issue Djuan any tickets for speeding and resisting arrest because she understands that it was an emergency situation *(page 151)*.
3. She has never met Djuan before and he is acting crazy, but she tells him to call Bob about a job opening for a mechanic *(page 150)*.
4. He finds out that it was not his fault that she died *(page 150)*.
5. Bob says he is hardworking, runs the station almost by himself, is helping with the repairs, and has earned a raise *(page 152)*.

EXERCISE 3—page 155

1. smart and not afraid of work
2. $3,600
3. one of the children is breathing harder and faster than the rest
4. has a fever, has difficulty breathing, and is delirious
5. $496, cash
6. 160 miles, three hours
7. $34
8. Jerry Rafsky, Paul Rafsky
9. ninety
10. handcuff him to a bed
11. dancing at the top of a parking structure

EXERCISE 4—pages 156-57

Here are some examples of synonyms and some sample sentences. If you're not sure of your synonym or your sentence, look the words up in a dictionary.

2. chance

   When she retires, I will have an <u>opportunity</u> for a promotion to supervisor.

3. divider

   Amy could see the top of Gigi's head above the <u>partition</u> in the ladies' room.

4. sensed

   My mother <u>detected</u> traces of chocolate chip cookies all over me.

5. urging

   Mark is <u>coaxing</u> the fish to bite by putting salami on his hook.

6. more and more

   Day by day, I become <u>increasingly</u> certain that the vice president is an egomaniac.

7. surprised

   Tim was <u>startled</u> to find that Elizabeth had hidden in the back seat of his car all the way from New Haven, Connecticut.

8. bought

   Kyle <u>purchased</u> a partridge in a pear tree for his true love.

9. counted

   I <u>tallied</u> the number of times the copy machine broke down last week, and the total was forty-seven.

10. honest

    Give me a <u>straight</u> answer, buster, or you've had it.

11. checklist

    The <u>inventory</u> of her personal possessions shows that she owned seventeen Bibles.

12. soon

    Miles will be with you to take your order <u>momentarily</u>.

13. steady

    They fight all the time, but their marriage is actually <u>stable</u> and loving.

EXERCISE 5—pages 168-69

You may not have chosen the same pieces of evidence that are listed below. Make sure that your pieces of evidence really support the statement and that they actually appear in the reading.

	Jill	Liz
1. a.	agreeable, lets Ted lead	always challenged Ted
b.	conventional life structured by sorority	unconventional
c.	soft in appearance and manner	slim and athletic

2. a. He thinks to himself that he has entered a world of plastic people. He compares the people in a country club to mannequins.

   b. Something deep inside him tells him to get in his car and leave the cottage.

3. a. She works very hard at something she is committed to.

   b. She works alongside the carpenters who are building her model, and she seems completely at ease with them.

4. a. Sam is afraid to sleep alone.

   b. He asks when Josh is coming back.

5. a. Many of the characters come to visit her at the Candy Hut.

   b. Djuan allows his daughter to work for her.

   c. Liz comes back to renew her old friendship with her.

6. a. Djuan writes a letter to the police department and gets Rita a commendation.

   b. He sends Rita flowers.

7. a. He has recently finished part of a training program.

   b. He is going to specialize in front-end work at Bob's second station.

EXERCISE 6—page 169

a.	2	e.	5
b.	3	f.	7
c.	4	g.	6
d.	1		

EXERCISE 7—page 170

1.	F	8.	F
2.	F	9.	F
3.	F	10.	T
4.	F	11.	F
5.	T	12.	T
6.	F	13.	F
7.	T		

EXERCISE 8—page 170

You may not have answered these questions in the same way as the answers given below. Review your explanations and evidence to be sure you really answered the question.

1. When he is loading his car, he sees headlights coming and panics, thinking someone is coming after him. This leads him to an irrational action: he takes off as fast as he can, abandoning some of his things. Then he causes damage to his car, two parked cars, and the oncoming car. Of course, the oncoming car has nothing to do with him—it has an ordinary family in it.

2. Ted might prefer to marry Jill because Jill is easier to deal with than Liz—Jill is easygoing and sweet while Liz was challenging and unconventional. Ted realizes that Jill is always agreeable and lets him lead, but Liz always challenged him. In fact, Ted thinks to himself, "I don't want such a strong-headed woman as Liz anyway."

3. Answers will vary.

4. a. Rita says that as long as Josh can't settle down with one woman, she and Josh can only be friends.

   b. Their friendship seems to be based on their ability to talk easily and have fun together, as well as their mutual love for Sam. Also, they have always been physically attracted to each other, which must add some spice to their friendship.

5. Perhaps they care about each other because they have been through so much together and because they helped each other in bad times. Rita saved Marissa's life. Bob and Carol gave Djuan a good job with a future. Shirley helped Liz find a place to help people by telling her about the Agency for Battered Women, and Liz was able to counsel Rita. Experiences like these would have to bring people close together.